MAKING PRAYER REAL

LYNN JAMES RADCLIFFE

MAKING
PRAYER
REAL

ABINGDON PRESS

New York • Nashville

MAKING PRAYER REAL

Copyright MCMLII by Pierce and Smith

Library of Congress Catalog Card Number: 52-8839

PRINTED AND BOUND AT NASHVILLE,
TENNESSEE, UNITED STATES OF AMERICA

PREFACE

"OH THAT I KNEW WHERE I MIGHT FIND HIM!" THESE WORDS OF Job spoken centuries ago might well have been said by a Christian of today. To this ageless yearning of the human heart Jeremiah makes answer: "And ye shall seek me, and find me, when ye shall search for me with all your heart."

Our consciousness of God has grown dim as we have advanced into the twentieth century, but man cannot long be satisfied cut off from the Source of his being. Especially is this so when the foundations of civilization tremble and shake. Instinctively man reaches out after the Eternal and seeks to renew vital contact with the Divine. Today there is a deep stirring of many hearts and the starting out of many people in search of some highway that will lead them toward God. Perhaps not for many generations have there been so many who deeply desire to find some way for making prayer real.

The trail which this book seeks to mark out is not my personal discovery, though I have tried humbly to follow along on it and, so far as my spirit had the power, to enjoy the full wonder of it. It is a well-worn path over which the saints of the ages have walked. I have sought merely to gather up the legacy of the most valid experiences of the great Christian men and women of prayer who have gone before us. I have tried to make available for our use today the literature of devotion and the experience in prayer which is our classic heritage through the ecumenical Church. This has been kept alive in the hearts of true Christians in all the centuries since our Master walked on earth. The universal Church holds in common everything that meets the high standard of being in conformity with the spirit and teaching of Jesus. We may think of the Church as a wheel. The nearer we are to the hub or center—Jesus Christ our Lord—the closer we draw together. As the spokes radiate from the center toward the periphery, they become farther apart. In all matters of essential faith, of prayer and devotion, and of Christlike living and action, we are at the very heart of ecumenical Christianity. When Christians devoutly pray, they are one in spirit and in practice.

The way of prayer suggested here is more than the presentation of techniques. Prayer at its deepest is the very heart of religion itself. It is man aware of and interacting with the living Presence of God. It cannot be divorced from our faith, our practice of the highest Christian ethics, or our working with God to bring in His Kingdom. In other words, true Christian prayer is intellectually, morally, and socially conditioned. The Christian life of devotion includes and motivates the Christian life of action. It is an organic process. The prayer experience and the process of life adjustment to the will of God go hand in hand—that is, if they are truly Christian. Along with this we must remember that the basic laws of real prayer are the effective principles of healthy-mindedness. Whenever this is not true, we can be sure that we have deviated from the Christian pathway of prayer. The result of the highest forms of prayer should be a more perfect integration of the personality for more effective living and more powerful action.

There are no short cuts in prayer. Techniques in themselves are not enough. I have therefore endeavored to outline as clearly as possible the various stages in the prayer process and the objectives of the great movements of the spirit as we turn toward God. If we can be true to the spirit of these approaches, we shall, each of us, gradually develop personal methods of praying that are most helpful to us as individuals. However, there are many classical methods of prayer with which we should become familiar. Their use by those not now acquainted with them will take time, effort, and devotion. Sometimes the acts described will not prove immediately helpful, but we should persevere in their use, for they have the approval of centuries of Christian experience. We must not cut ourselves off from their benefits by discarding them before we have mastered them. Again, we must not try to change everything at once; we must retain enough of our familiar habits of prayer to keep the experience satisfying and real. We must, however, seek to get out of any ruts in our prayer habits. We should open our minds to the stimulus of new ways of praying. We should pay the price in soul discipline of growing constantly in our prayer practices.

We should also be aware that we cannot enjoy some of the higher stages of prayer until we have first mastered its initial disciplines. One would not expect to unlock the treasures of literature in a foreign language without prior training in its grammar and vocabulary, and without some personal experience in its usage. Nor would one expect to take a seminar in some university subject without first having passed the basic courses. Even so is prayer. Weeks and months spent on vocal and mental prayer may be necessary before one may come to understand, in the only way in which one can ever understand, the high meaning of contemplative prayer. May I therefore suggest that, after becoming familiar with the whole sweep of the developing life of prayer, you return to one chapter and endeavor practically and devotedly to make it a part of your own living experience.

It is my earnest hope that this book shall be not so much read as lived. May God's Holy Spirit take its words, imperfect and human as they are, to move your soul toward Him and to help you in making prayer real.

LYNN JAMES RADCLIFFE

Hyde Park Community Methodist Church
Cincinnati, Ohio

CONTENTS

11

PART THREE

The Way of Spiritual Discipline

CONTENTS

PART FIVE

The Way of Oneness with God

CONTENTS

PART ONE

Preludes to Prayer

CHAPTER I

Wanted: A Spiritual Renaissance!

AWAKENING—IN THE CHRISTIAN CHURCH

Awake, awake; put on thy strength, O Zion.
—Isa. 52:1

IT WAS A SUMMER EVENING IN THE GREAT MUSIC SHED AT Tanglewood in the Berkshires. Ten thousand people had gathered to hear the music of Brahms. On the platform were arranged the members of the Boston Symphony Orchestra, and before them stood one of the great conductors of our age, the late Serge Koussevitzky.

There was a moment of poised waiting as with lifted baton he fronted his orchestra. They were his friends; he knew every one of them intimately. He knew he could count upon their unfailing response. In the soul of the conductor the great symphony was already surging into life. He knew every modulation of it, every theme in the development of the succeeding movements. Already it had begun to call for release in his soul.

Then the moment came; all was in readiness. In one masterful downbeat the baton fell. Instantly the orchestra thrilled into beauty, the beauty of a great symphony masterfully played. As the music progressed, every expectancy of the conductor met with the alerted response of the prepared orchestra: a wave of his hand, and instantly twenty violins playing as one swept into surging song; the lift of a finger, and the woodwinds gave back the melody against the vibrant bass; a quick-flung glance, and the French horn sounded forth; a decisive gesture, and the beat of the drum made rhythmic answer. The conductor became the fusing point where the beauty of the symphony flamed into living sound. How eagerly Koussevitzky called for their response! The perspiration stood out upon his forehead. His face was working with the intent passion of his desire to release the perfection of beauty.

Strangely and unaccountably, as I watched the conductor and the orchestra, another scene swept before my mind—Christ confronting His people, calling for their response to His dreams, as He stood on the Mount of Olives in far-off Judea on the first Palm Sunday. He reached out His hands in the urgency of His entreaty for response, lifted His face with the passion of God glowing in it for the music of the Kingdom. Now was the appointed time. These were His people. He knew them intimately. They knew the symphony. They were prepared by ages of familiarity with the music of God. With one masterful downbeat the Master on the mountaintop gave the signal for God's symphony to be played. . . . But there was no answer, no response. Only tense silence from the temple! Then raucous cacophony from the people, blasphemous discords, assertive dissonances, selfish disharmonies—mounting up into an awful climax in the staccato drumbeats of the hammers that crucified Him.

Suddenly it came to me that it was not back there in Palestine; it was here and now that the Master waited. It was now that we did not see Him or hear Him. Always before us stands the great Christ calling for our response. We have so mistaken reality. We are so immersed in other things. What is real? Our deep personality, our soul is real. Love, service, the Kingdom of God are real. The eternal spiritual world is real. God is real. Christ is real. And we never see Him ready to conduct the symphony for which God is waiting! Yet this is the basic reality of life—God confronting His children, appealing for their response. When we awaken to this reality and perceive the nearness of the Divine Presence, our spiritual development will enter a higher stage.

1. THE NEED FOR A RELIGIOUS ADVANCE TODAY

Ours is a godless age. It is not that so many people in the Western world are openly atheistic; it is rather that their God-consciousness has grown dim. God was real to our fathers, but to us He is vague and distant. There can be no vital religion until in some real sense a man comes face to face with his God.

The foundations of our faith have been shaken. The ground of our security trembles. Martin Buber says: "The bulwarks have fallen away, and the abyss is screaming." Where once our culture reared the proud monuments of a conquering civilization, tragedy has struck. Mankind is not sure whether history may "crush us with its turning heel." With the eclipse of our spiritual powers the subconscious and brutal forces have seized control.

We are now confronted with ultimate alternatives. Either we are akin to the Universe, to God, or we are alien to Him: a disturbing sense of spiritual alienation haunts our world. Either there is light upon the future pathway of our history from the eternal purposes of God, or we are hopeless: the gloom of pessimism darkens man's present outlook. Either there are resources of spiritual strength that can come to us from on high, or modern man is helpless: there is a fatalistic sense of impotence as man confronts the trampling march of coming doom. Either there is a realm of God and love which is eternal, or there is an abyss of nothingness: the quicksands of time on which we build have revealed that we have here no continuing city. We can build shelters against the A-bomb and assume that by dispersal we may escape its devastation, but the approach of human dissolution cannot be ultimately dodged.

Modern man has been uprooted from the great traditions of his faith and is now conscious of his profound dissociation. He is cut off from his eternal environment and from his God. As Edwin Arlington Robinson puts it:

21

> We set ourselves to grow
> In the wrong earth, and soon we had no roots.[1]

Archibald MacLeish in "The End of the World" strikingly pictures the nihilism of our modern outlook:

> And there, there overhead, there, there, hung over
> Those thousands of white faces, those dazed eyes,
> There in the starless dusk, the poise, the hover,
> There with vast wings across the canceled skies,
> There in the sudden blackness, the black pall
> Of nothing, nothing, nothing—nothing at all.[2]

This is the ultimate and most devastating of all the catastrophes that can ever happen to man. So long as there is hope, even the smallest possible glimmer, man can endure anything that can happen to him. But when all the lights go out, then he cannot stand it. He breaks under the impact. In this crisis of modern civilization man is reaching out in the dark, seeking to rediscover God. As perhaps not in many centuries, there is now desperately wanted—a spiritual renaissance.

2. NEW LIFE IN THE CHURCH

We need a powerful revival of fresh vitality in prayer, of renewed conviction in our faith, and of new life in the Church. Two or three generations ago there were more saints than there are now. The religious lives of Christians were more convincing to the world and more powerful in their influence. Today, as the Bishop of Dornakal in India has pointed out, the Church is spending too much of its energy in "taking permanent care of hereditary Christians." But whenever religion degenerates into a tired shuffle of old duties, the Spirit of God tends to break through, bringing an outburst of new life into the hearts of those who are prepared and sensitized to receive it.

[1] *Amaranth* (New York: The Macmillan Co., 1934), p. 16. Used by permission.
[2] *Streets in the Moon* (Boston: Houghton Mifflin Co., 1926). Used by permission.

Centuries ago Teresa of Avila pictured our progress in the spiritual life as a journey from one mansion to another in the interior castle of the soul. The general spirit of her classification still holds today. We may now speak of a large group of people who are dwelling in the first mansion. They are the "believing souls," people who are nominal members of the Christian Church. They are the new converts, the children, the habitual members, and also the backslidden Christians who once had known a higher life but who have now grown lukewarm and indifferent. Next there is the mansion of the "good Christian souls," those who have heard God calling them to come up higher. They pray morning and night. They are fighting their sins and living as good, respectable Christian people. They attend church, but their devotion is intermittent. Their interest comes and goes. They are sincere but inconstant. Then there is the third mansion, that of the "devout followers" of Christ. They are the advancing souls who desire spiritual progress. They really want to follow in His steps. They are regular in church attendance and interested in the work of the Kingdom. They enjoy spiritual reading and have a zest for prayer. They are tithers, and they practice self-denial. Their hearts are sometimes kindled by experiences of the Presence of the Living Christ. Then next there are in the fourth mansion the "fervent souls," the saints without whom any local church is impoverished, those whose lives evidence very humbly but sincerely an imitation of Christ, the apostles of today who are under the burden of the advancement of Christ's Kingdom, the men and women whose prayers of intercession are deep and powerful, the people who rise to the prayer of contemplation and "practice the Presence of God."

The spiritual renaissance which is needed today is an advance by many Christians to these higher mansions of the soul. Teresa pointedly asked those about her whether they were content to be dwarfs in the spiritual life, or whether they wanted to grow toward the fulfillment of their higher spiritual capacities. As we make answer today, the place to begin is in the life of prayer, for prayer is the very heart of religion itself. A quickening of the life of devotion is the supreme need of Christianity if it is to become the powerful force our modern world so desperately needs.

CHAPTER II

When New Life Breaks Through

AWAKENING—IN OUR PERSONAL EXPERIENCE

Awake thou that sleepest, . . . and Christ shall give thee light.
—Eph. 5:14

IF NEW LIFE IS TO COME THROUGH THE CHURCH TO BRING A renaissance of faith and hope to our age, it must begin in the lives of individual Christians. We must, each one of us, start out upon the highroad of prayer in a personal pilgrimage from self to God.

1. THE NATURE OF OUR AWAKENING

An inner awakening is the first classic movement in the symphony of prayer and devotion. It is man becoming aware of the eternal environment to which in reality he belongs. Evelyn Underhill defines it as a "sudden, intense, and joyous perception of God immanent in the universe; of the divine beauty and unutterable power and splendour of that richer life in which the individual is immersed, and of a new life to be lived by the self in correspondence with this now dominant fact of existence." [1]

This spiritual awakening that starts us on the highroad of prayer is not to be confused with conversion, which is assumed already to have taken place. In conversion we accept by faith the grace of God, revealed in Jesus Christ and made available through the action of the Holy Spirit within our souls. In some way we commit ourselves to Christ and to His way of life; we

[1] *Mysticism* (New York: E. P. Dutton & Co., 12th ed., 1930), p. 179. Used by permission.

25

are born again. In the Church in America today conversions of the Pauline type are not the way by which most church members have entered upon the Christian life. When such a conversion has occurred, it is possible that the spiritual awakening of which we are speaking may continue from that one experience. This, however, is not normally the case.

The way in which God's Spirit deals with us is an individual matter. The usual course of our development is this: After our entrance upon the Christian life, we continue to grow in grace and in the knowledge of God. As we advance in our spiritual nurture, there comes a growing awareness of how far short we have come of the glory of God. We become wistful for a closer walk with Him, a truly radiant experience, a more real contact with His power and His love. However, we dimly realize what a more living religion would involve. We recognize that it would be costly. We are attracted, and yet we are inhibited by fear, by self-interest, and by crowd pressure. Augustine said, "I was swept up to Thee by Thy beauty, and torn away from Thee by my own weight." [2]

There comes a period of struggle and inner conflict. We are dissatisfied with our spiritual lives. We have broken with the world, become a member of the Church, and committed ourselves to the way of Christ; but we have not become Christians with power in our lives, fruitfulness in our influence, and radiance in our personal experience of God's living Presence. We spend years debating whether or not we shall give ourselves wholly to God. We hold back; we procrastinate; we temporize. But all the while in our hearts there is the sense of God's inescapable nearness and appealing love. We know all too well what we are doing in our Christian lives, but we also know what He is doing. His eyes are fixed upon us with unchangeable love. We cry out, "Why dost Thou ever remember me, while I so often forget Thee?" We sense that our prayer life is haphazard and inadequate. Without prayer as a living communion with God "faith remains a theoretical conviction;

[2] *Confessions*, Bk. VII, ch. xvii.

26

worship is only an external and formal act; moral action is without spiritual depth; man remains at a distance from God." [3]

Then the Spirit of God breaks through. The veil between the visible and the invisible is drawn asunder; we come to an unforgettable moment of awakening; new life floods into our souls; prayer becomes real; God's nearness is felt; and we start out joyously to practice the Presence of God. This new awakening, which dispels the lukewarmness of our religion and illumines us with the divine fire, comes to many people in the immediateness of one definite experience. Others grow slowly, without any marked crisis, into this living consciousness of the Divine. However it may come, beyond all things else our lives need this awakening to the Presence of God and the consequent deepening of our lives of prayer.

John Wesley's experience at Aldersgate Street was a conversion, but it was, at the same time, an awakening. He had long been a follower of Christ. Now his religion flamed into reality; his heart was strangely warmed. He felt that he really did trust in Christ and Christ alone for his salvation. Through the open channel of his new life God began to work mightily.

Blaise Pascal, the great French mathematician and philosopher, had had, a century earlier, his own spiritual awakening. The secret of his life was revealed when, after his death, a fragment of parchment was found sewed in his doublet. On it there was a rough drawing of the cross and the joyous phrases that outlined the impact of Reality upon his soul. Trying to express the inexpressible radiance that had illumined his heart in these high hours he said, "From half-past ten till half-past twelve, Fire!" The phrases that follow are abrupt and broken but they convey the impression of a profound spiritual experience. Himself a great scholar and philosopher, he now cries out in amazement, "Not the God of philosophers and of scholars! . . . Certitude! Certitude! Joy! Peace! . . . The world has not known Thee, but *I* have known Thee . . . Joy! Joy! Joy! Abun-

---

[3] Friedrich Heiler, *Prayer* (London and New York: Oxford University Press, 1932) , p. 362. Used by permission.

dance of Joy!" The Presence means so much to him that when he feels the fire beginning to die down he cries: "Are You departing from me? Oh, let me not be separated from You eternally!" It is now unendurable that he should live without the vision of this radiant Presence. His final act is a giving of himself totally to God in complete surrender. It was this, doubtless, to which he referred in his classic words: "The heart has reasons that the reason knows not of."

Brother Lawrence's awakening was of an entirely different kind, but just as convincing. From the moment that the reality of God's Presence dawned upon his consciousness, he joyously practiced the Presence of God.

"He told me," says the anonymous reporter of the conversations, "that God had done him a singular favor in his conversion at the age of eighteen. That in the winter, seeing a tree stripped of its leaves, and considering that within a little time the leaves would be renewed, and after that the flowers and fruit appear, he received a high view of the Providence and Power of God, which has never since been effaced from his soul. That this view had set him perfectly loose from the world and kindled in him such a love for God that he could not tell whether it had increased during the more than forty years he had lived since." [4]

Just as in his case, so we find that the spiritual awakening frequently comes to youth as they, on the verge of manhood and womanhood, feel an urgent call to enter into a life of more real communion and contact with God. It does not matter how simply or how dramatically they come to this supreme moment. The tremendous need today is for awakened souls, aglow with the light and joy of a new, personal vision of God.

Concerning this Emily Herman writes:

Through all the centuries men and women have been awakened to see that the world—yes, and the Church also—was dying for lack of prayer. Always and everywhere apostles of prayer have arisen, calling upon a materialised Church to cease from the busy-

[4] *The Practice of the Presence of God,* First Conversation.

ness of merely institutional activities and give herself to the true business of prayer. At every great crisis in the world's history multitudes have re-discovered the secret of prayer, and a tidal wave of petition and intercession has swept through Christendom. But again and again, once the crisis was past and the tension slackened, the voice of prayer became faint and inarticulate, and soon there was only a thin trickle where once the flood had been. Today . . . we have once more become acutely conscious of the need for prayer.[5]

2. REDISCOVERING THE HEART OF PRAYER

Prayer flourishes in most healthy form in the prepared soil of a great religion. When Isaiah had his tremendous vision in the temple and was able to say, "I saw also the Lord, . . . high and lifted up," and to hear the cry of the seraphim, "Holy, holy, holy, is the Lord of hosts: the whole earth is full of His glory," the experience flowered forth from the deeply rooted faith in which for years he had been nurtured. An age of great faith is apt to produce an awakening of powerful prayer.

When we pray, therefore, it is necessary that we be—in William James's phrase—"tough-minded" enough to affirm and experience the reality of the faith which we hold. Believing in the personality of God the Father Almighty, in Christ Jesus His only Son our Lord, and in the Holy Spirit, we move on from this assurance to actual contact and communion with the Living Presence of the eternal God. The characteristic of such an experience is its overtone of reality. Somehow we know that we are in touch with the Divine. We pray in the certitude that we are not alone; God is with us. The heart of prayer is this conviction that we are not speaking words out into an unanswering void, but speaking, or thinking, in the very Presence of God. All true prayer includes some recognition, however dim, of this reference to the reality of God's living nearness.

Many people have believed that our awareness of God is primarily emotional. Because our feelings are notoriously un-

[5] *Creative Prayer* (New York: George H. Doran Co., 1925), pp. 14-15. Used by permission of Harper & Bros.

stable, our experience of God has been thought to fluctuate in relation to their intensity. But strong, rugged convictions provide a far more stable basis for our awareness of the Divine than do our feelings. Almost always there are, in fact, emotional overtones, but these are secondary and not primary. The foundation fact in religious experience is not the intensity of our emotions, but the profundity of our convictions. The winds of emotion may fill the lifted sails, but a reasoned faith must serve as the rudder if we are to avoid capsizing or pursuing a very erratic course. What Christians through the ages have believed about God is the reality which we seek to discover in the vividness of our personal experience when we turn Godward in prayer.

One time I was discussing prayer with E. Stanley Jones. He had pointed out that there was something vital lacking in the praying of Indian mystics. He had commented that their attempts to pray were sincere, and their techniques of prayer were highly developed, and yet there was something still missing. At last he put his finger upon it and said: "They struggle so hard to find God, but oh, their concept of God is so thin." They have not had the privilege of beholding the glory of God in the face of Jesus Christ.

3. MAKING CONTACT WITH THE DIVINE PRESENCE

a. God the Father Almighty. Throughout the ages men and women have been passing beyond a faith in God and an assurance that God is a Presence near us always to the supreme awakening in a personal contact between their lives and the living God as they prayed. The psalmist said, "O God," and then went beyond to say, "Thou art my God." The prophet said: "Lift up thy voice with strength; lift it up, be not afraid; say unto the cities of Judah, Behold your God." (Isa. 40:9.) But then he awakened to a personal realization in which the assertions of faith flamed into the living realities of a firsthand encounter with God. He heard God speaking directly to him personally and saying: "Fear thou not; for I am with thee."

(Isa. 41:10.) The Bible abounds in accounts of these soul-stirring experiences which are at the very heart of our religion:

And Jacob called the name of the place Peniel: for I have seen God face to face, and my life is preserved. (Gen. 32:30.)

And the Lord spake unto Moses face to face, as a man speaketh unto his friend. (Exod. 33:11.)

And after the earthquake a fire; but the Lord was not in the fire: and after the fire a still small voice. And it was so, when Elijah heard it, that he wrapped his face in his mantle, and went out, and stood in the entering in of the cave. And, behold, there came a voice unto him, and said, What doest thou here, Elijah? (I Kings 19: 12-13.)

Whither shall I go from thy spirit? or whither shall I flee from thy presence? (Ps. 139:7.)

Continuously in all generations men and women have thus awakened to a personal contact with the living Presence of God. Sometimes this occurs in an hour of crisis, sometimes in a moment of exaltation, but most frequently as the soul of man reaches toward the Divine in prayer. Such a moment came to Richard Byrd during the ordeal of his solitary sojourn at the advance base in Antarctica. You recall how he tells in his book *Alone*[6] of weeks and months he spent amid the rigors of polar weather in which the thermometer dropped to eighty below zero. He got along fairly well until a small gasoline engine used in connection with his radio gave forth carbon monoxide fumes. He was made seriously ill, and found himself battling for his very life—alone, far from all human help, fronting terrific odds. It was an epic battle for survival. He was down to the last vestiges of those ultimate reserves of strength that sustain bare existence. He dared to keep the oilstove alight for only short periods. The deadening cold pressed in; the frost line crept farther down the walls. His strength was ebbing.

[6] New York: G. P. Putnam's Sons, 1938.

He could not eat. He was critically ill. No outside resources could get to him. No machines and no human beings could cross the miles to him through that wall of paralyzing cold.

Crushed to his knees by that dark coalition of circumstances, he reached out for God's help—as man always does in an ultimate hour. He was not a mystic; he had not regarded himself as an unusually religious man. But he had a rigorous mind, logical and decisive. He began to think as clearly and as cogently as he had ever done in his life. He said to himself, "The universe is not dead. Therefore, there is an Intelligence there, and it is all-pervading. . . . The human race, then, is not alone in the universe. Though I am cut off from human beings, *I am not alone*."

It was a reasoned, logical approach. But now that at last he needed such insight, it came clearly and strongly. He had a sense of the Universe backing him up in his fight for life. Slowly he pushed back the black wings of approaching death and the icy breath of the miasmas of fear and began a fight that does credit to the latent heroism in the hearts of men. And he won through. As early as it was possible, and long before it was safe, members of his expedition came to his rescue. But the victory had already been won, by one man, alone, with the unseen power of God backing him up. The decisive step in our awakening can be such a personal discovery of the relevance in our lives of some great conviction of our faith.

To grow deeply quiet and then to repeat slowly, thoughtfully, and reverently, "I believe in God the Father Almighty," can bring to any one of us new reality as we pray. To repeat the opening words of the Lord's Prayer with sincere and reverent insight may help us to awaken to the tremendous faith which they enshrine: "Our Father"—the infinite and universal God of love, . . . "who art in heaven"—the Almighty Ruler of the universe, . . . "hallowed be Thy name"—the holy, awesome Being at the heart of Reality; . . . "Thy kingdom come"—the powerful Providence that is working through all the events of history to accomplish His dream; . . . "Thy will be done"—

the God who cares for us and holds a purpose in His great heart for our lives and for our daily needs; to Him we turn with growing faith and kindling vision.

b. *The Living Christ*. The early Church was born in the experience of the Living Christ. They believed the words: "I am he that liveth, and was dead; and, behold, I am alive for evermore." (Rev. 1:18.) Of the experiences of Stephen, the first martyr, it was written: "But he, being full of the Holy Ghost, looked up stedfastly into heaven, and saw the glory of God, and Jesus standing on the right hand of God, and said, Behold, I see the heavens opened, and the Son of man standing on the right hand of God." (Acts 7:55-56.)

It was an arresting experience of the Presence of the Living Christ that transformed the life of Paul: "And as he journeyed, he came near Damascus: and suddenly there shined round about him a light from heaven: and he fell to the earth, and heard a voice saying unto him, Saul, Saul, why persecutest thou me? And he said, Who art thou, Lord? And the Lord said, I am Jesus whom thou persecutest." (Acts 9:3-5.)

The Christian community started in the Upper Room at Jerusalem on the first Easter evening. The group of disciples had assembled there. Mary came in and told them of her tremendous experience in the garden that morning. "Jesus is alive!" she cried. "I have seen Him." There came a quick knock at the door. When they were assured that those who wished to enter were friends, they opened the door and the two who had been on a journey to Emmaus came in. With radiant faces they told how they had been in the presence of Jesus and had been made aware of this new eternal realm which was so near to them. While they were all talking eagerly together, suddenly came Jesus, a Living Presence, and stood in the midst of them. Their talk abruptly ceased; their awe deepened into fear. Then Jesus spoke: "Peace! Peace be unto you!" A great stillness filled the room. Then as they saw that it was really He—the same intimate, loving, understanding Companion, there in living actuality before them—they were filled with unutterable joy.

33

In the forty days and nights after Easter, Jesus kept appearing to His followers again and again. His disciples came to know that, wherever they were and whatever they were doing, the Living Christ was ever close by their side. At any moment He might appear. They came to know that He was always there. When Jesus had completed this revelation and had established this unshakable foundation for their faith in His Living Presence, He was parted from them in the Ascension. The last words that His lips ever spoke to them were these: "Lo, I am with you alway, even unto the end of the world." (Matt. 28:20.)

There are some facts so tremendous that they have only to be demonstrated once in order to be established forever. Even if we do not have the full spiritual experience of this reality, surely every Christian can intellectually accept the facts. This is a part of the living creed of Christianity. Awakening to this tremendous truth profoundly deepens our prayer life. His Presence is real. That same Jesus is alive forevermore. He is here now. *Christ is alive!*

c. The Holy Spirit. To the early Christian community there came another basic spiritual revelation. At Pentecost the Holy Spirit was revealed in the majesty and mystery and power of His indwelling Presence. The universal testimony of the Church throughout the ages is that He is ever speaking deep in the center of our souls. This again is not merely an emotion; it is rather the direct experience of the mysterious, tremendous, awesome Presence of the very Spirit of God dwelling within us, acting upon our spirits and making us aware of God's eternal nearness. The Holy Spirit proceeds from God the Father and from Christ the Saviour, eternally of their nature and one with them. The warm reality of God as revealed in Christ lives in the personality of the Holy Spirit. Whenever a man awakens to a consciousness of the inner light of this indwelling Spirit, his prayer life is forever transformed.

> Spirit Creative, brooding still
> Where unformed worlds await Thy will,

Where chaos hides the light of day
From men unyielded to Thy sway;

Brood o'er Thy Church, Creative Word,
Until our souls are strangely stirred,
Until there dawns what man had lost—
The mighty power of Pentecost.[7]

One time, in the early days of television, I was preaching over a station in Cincinnati. A friend in a city thirty miles away had a new set. Without knowing what program was being televised, he tuned in. Later he told me how startling it was to see me suddenly appear in his room and begin to talk as if I were really there. Why should it then be deemed incredible that God, who creates and energizes the electronic realm, can likewise in the spiritual realm sensitize His children to His Living Presence? It is an awakening in some way, in any way, to this tremendous fact that is the precondition of making prayer real.

God is here now as you read these words. He is in the room with you as truly as He was in the Upper Room on Easter night, as truly as on the day of Pentecost, as truly as on Mount Sinai.

God is one in His eternal substance, three in the eternal personalities of which His one life eternally consists. Sometimes in experience we focus with awe and adoration on one personality, sometimes on another. There is no confusion in our understanding of the oneness of God, and there is infinite richness in our reverent contacts with Him as Father, Son, and Holy Spirit.

This joyous perception of God as immanent and real begins to illumine our lives. Later the vision will grow in reality and in power. But now we have had a moment of abrupt intuition and in some way have experienced the breaking through of the Divine. The veil of eternity has parted, and we have glimpsed the awesome Presence of God.

[7] From "Hymn for the Living Church," by L. J. R.

Yet ever and anon a trumpet sounds
From the hid battlements of Eternity;
Those shaken mists a space unsettle, then
Round the half-glimpsèd turrets slowly wash again.
    But not ere him who summoneth
    I first have seen.[8]

It is this experience to which Jesus called us to look forward when he said, "The hour cometh, and now is, when the true worshippers shall worship the Father in spirit and in truth: for the Father seeketh such to worship him." (John 4:23.) God is seeking us, and we awaken to hear His call. Meister Eckhart says: "Thou needest not call Him to thee from a distance; thy opening and His entering are but one moment; it is harder for Him to wait, than for thee." [9]

May we, whatever our spiritual experience in the past has been, awaken now to a still deeper contact with the Living Presence of the eternal God. Inspired by His Spirit, may we be moved to undertake the disciplines and to enter upon the pilgrimage that will lead us to new heights of oneness with Him in prayer and to new adventures of Christlike living in growing adjustment to His revealed will. May this be for each one of us a moment of response that will enable God to use us in helping to bring to our world that spiritual renaissance for which our Master now is waiting.

[8] Francis Thompson, "The Hound of Heaven."
[9] Quoted in Underhill, *Mysticism.*

CHAPTER III

A Way to Mastery

DISCIPLINE—IN PRAYER

Strait is the gate, and narrow is the way, which leadeth unto life.
—Matt. 7:14

THE WAY TO MASTERY IN ANY REALM IS THROUGH DISCIPLINED living. Our age has largely forgotten this and is continually seeking short cuts to the millennium and easy techniques for spiritual living; but, while our modern generation may seek for tramways or ski lifts, the saints of the ages knew that only the long, steady, determined climb up the trail leads to the spiritual heights.

This, I believe, was what the Master meant when He said: "Strait is the gate, and narrow is the way, which leadeth unto life, and few there be that find it." He knew that there was a price for all great living. Life must narrow down in concentration upon some worthy goal. It must pass through gateways with a decisiveness that dares to open and close them. But this is no negative thing. It is not a matter of losing the joy and zest and fullness of life; it is rather finding something of such surpassing value that we let go of our marginal concerns in order that we may gain it. No man has lost his life who is pursuing a high goal with all his heart. But the demanding heights are costly, and the price of all real achievement is controlled devotion.

In every realm this is so. We do not drift upward toward mastery in art. The creative process here, too, demands discipline. The facility of a master craftsman is bought with a price.

Holman Hunt was once in his studio with a group of young artist friends. Anyone who has ever been in the little chapel at Keble College in Oxford, where his masterpiece, "The Light of the World," confronts us with Christ knocking upon the door, has felt the powerful impact of his artistry. On this occasion the artist stepped up to his blank canvas and with one sure, swift stroke inscribed a perfect circle, so perfect that the brush mark was everywhere of even width and the meeting place of beginning and ending could scarcely be detected. One of the young women in the group, believing that there was some trick or knack to such a feat, exclaimed, "Oh, Mr. Hunt, I should like to be able to do that. How do you do it?" For answer, the artist smiled and said, "It is perfectly simple, madam. All one has to do is to practice eight hours a day for forty years."

Mastery in music is just as costly. Hans Kindler, who was for many years the distinguished conductor of the National Symphony Orchestra in Washington, D. C., told one time of an experience which he had while traveling in Switzerland. As he was walking through one of the reception halls in a resort hotel, he suddenly was arrested by the sound of Beethoven's *Appassionata Sonata* being played masterfully in the adjacent music room. In a moment, however, the flood of beauty stopped abruptly, and the unseen player went back and practiced one phrase over and over again until he was finally satisfied with it. Then he swept on in his thrilling interpretation of great music. Once again he stopped and worked over a phrase until he had perfected it to his own demanding standards. After a little while Hans Kindler moved to the doorway and looked in. There sat the aged Paderewski, one of the greatest masters of the music of Beethoven of his time, still practicing for perfection in the field of his art.

It is not luck that enables the halfback to fling the winning touchdown pass in the closing seconds of a hard football game. Through months and years he has trained his muscles and drilled his perceptions for this supreme moment. It was not by chance that Thomas Jefferson wrote the Declaration of Independence. Through years of study of Latin and Greek, classic history, and mankind's struggle for liberty through the ages he had prepared himself with a disciplined knowledge of freedom that uniquely equipped him for the great event when the opportunity came. What is thus true in every realm is supremely true regarding prayer. The way to mastery here too is through disciplined living.

1. THE DISCIPLINE OF TIME

Ever since Arnold Bennett wrote his disturbing essay *How to Live on Twenty-four Hours a Day,* we have been forced to realize that our problem is not lack of time but rather the disciplined control of time. Every man who ever lives has the same amount of time—twenty-four hours a day. To learn how to master our schedules so that we do not become the victims of impulse, or pressure, but rather make room for life's vital concerns is our basic problem. When a man says, "I am too busy to pray," what he is really saying is that he regards everything else in his day as of more value than prayer, and thus permits it to be crowded out. As we awaken to the reality of the Living Presence of God and the challenging possibility of making personal contact with Him, prayer becomes for us so vital that we make room for it by decisive planning and disciplined practice.

A very sincere Christian minister, a missionary who had served five years in Peiping, China, was associated with me at the old Tremont Street Church in Boston. He was making the most of his furlough in America by completing his education at Boston University School of Theology and at the same time gaining experience in pastoral work. Under the pressure of his studies, his ministerial duties, and his home responsibilities, every hour of his day became crowded. By imperceptible stages prayer was edged out of his schedule.

One day he was walking along the Esplanade beside the Charles River. As he walked, he had time to think over his life and to achieve a sense of real direction. Suddenly and insistently there dawned the consciousness of the way in which he was drifting.

"Here I am preparing myself as a missionary to China," he said to himself. "I am having many marvelous opportunities to enlarge my outlook and to strengthen my knowledge, but the main thing I have to take back with me, my consciousness of God, is growing dim. I have been forgetting to pray. The other concerns of life have crowded out prayer."

Then, having awakened to what was really happening to him, he made a quick decision. He promised God that he would never begin another day until he had taken time to become aware of God's nearness and had caught some intimation of His will for him in the new day.

"I felt much better after I had faced this thing and made my decision," he said, as he told me the experience at the end of the week. "I had promised God, and the matter was settled. I knew I was upon the right track again. Then I plunged into my work with new energy, but I was carrying a heavy schedule. That night a term paper had to be completed. I sat up until two o'clock getting it done. The next morning I slept as late as I could, hurriedly dressed, and went down to breakfast with just time for a hasty meal before rushing to my first class. Just as I sat down at the table, I suddenly recalled the experience of the day before, and here I was caught in the crush of circumstances on the very first morning. But those moments the day before had been very real to me. I just couldn't break faith with my promise. I hesitated just a moment, looking at the breakfast before me, then I pushed my chair back, went upstairs to my room again, took time for prayer, and went directly to school." I can still hear his chuckle as he added whimsically, "You know, the next morning I got up in time for breakfast, too."

It is some such seriousness of purpose which must lay hold of us if prayer is to become a reality in our lives. We have to come face to face with the fact that no techniques of prayer, no familiarity with books about prayer, can ever take the place of prayer itself. There is only one way in which we can ever make prayer real to ourselves, and that is by taking time at any cost each day for prayer. We must, every one of us, come to grips with ourselves at this point first. We must make prayer an affair of decision and character. It is not so much a matter of how long we pray, at first, but rather the setting apart of some definite period to be a parenthesis of the spirit cut out of the busy stream of life. This is an inescapable condition of real prayer.

In Moffatt's translation of Ezekiel there is this significant verse, "When you are dividing up the land you must set apart a sacred district for the Eternal." (Ezek. 45:1.)

> Let us put by some hour of every day
> For holy things!—whether it be when dawn
> Peers through the window pane, or when the noon
> Flames, like a burnished topaz, in the vault,
> Or when the thrush pours in the ear of eve
> Its plaintive monody; some little hour
> Wherein to hold rapt converse with the soul,
> From sordidness and self a sanctuary,
> Swept by the winnowing of unseen wings,
> And touched by the White Light Ineffable! [1]

We cannot possibly pray while we are torn between other duties that are competing for our time and attention. The prayer period must be God's time, sacred and set apart. Within this established time for devotion let the soul be free and un-trammeled by any other concerns. This is absolutely essential to the whole quality of the experience. This is a valid psychological principle for all of life—the disciplining and budgeting of our time so that in any particular segment we concentrate our entire attention upon one thing, the business at hand. Many of us are worn and tired by the inner nerve strain of never really enjoying any one thing that we do. The tension and psychological turmoil within us often come from the vain

[1] Clinton Scollard, "Sanctuary." Used by permission.

41

attempt to do one task while at the same time we feel the relentless demand of other tasks that clamor and compete for that same moment of our attention. In the place of prayer we discover that the setting apart of periods of purposeful action is one of the releasing disciplines of life. Even if the time must necessarily be brief, we must set it apart sacredly.

2. FIVE DAILY PRAYER PERIODS

Everyone should establish for himself a definite rule of prayer, and then he should carry it out with undeviating devotion. As a concrete suggestion, might we not observe the following five prayer periods as a minimum rule for personal devotions?

a. Awakening Prayer. Our first conscious thought belongs to God. After we subconsciously shut off the alarm clock, or answer the voice that awakens us, we turn immediately toward some brief, quickening experience of God's Presence. We do not now offer a long prayer, but we habitually place the consciousness of God as the initial experience of every day. If we awaken to find the spring sun streaming through our window and all the world laughing with beauty, then with a rush of gladness we thank Him for the glory of another day fresh from His creative hand. On the other hand, if we awaken to the consciousness that the day will bring heavy responsibilities and many burdens, then, before these assail us or our spirits become tense, we quietly reach out to sense the power of the Almighty and the peace of His Presence. We may offer a brief, conversational prayer, or we may simply grow quiet in wordless prayer, laying hold of the steady reality of His nearness. Muriel Lester says concerning this awakening prayer: "Let your whole self become conscious of him. Think of him as shining beauty, radiant joy, creative power, all-pervading love, perfect understanding, purity, and serenity. This need only take a moment or two once the habit has been formed, but it is of inestimable importance. It sets the tone for the whole day." [2]

[2] *Ways of Praying* (Nashville: Cokesbury Press), p. 7.

b. Morning Devotions. Sometime before the man leaves home
for business, or the woman plunges into the tasks of the day,
there should be a time set apart for the major period of
prayer. In the rush of the morning scramble, which has become so habitual for Americans, this prayer time has been
largely crowded out of our schedule. As simple an act as aris-
ing fifteen minutes, or more, earlier than usual to allow time for
our morning devotions would have a more revolutionary effect
upon our spiritual experience and our psychological well-being
than any other discipline we might undertake. It would enable
us to enter upon the day with a serenity and poise that could
not but increase our effectiveness. At the same time we should
have established a silent sanctuary of the soul where prayer
might become for each of us a living reality. It is in this period
that we should find our best opportunity to begin to practice
the life of devotion which will be presented in the subsequent
chapters of this book. Without such sacred times of regular
prayer, of what value are all our theories?

c. Noontide Prayer. Sometime in the middle of the day we
need a momentary pause in which to turn our thoughts Godward
in prayer. It may be that this prayer will have to be offered
with open eyes, while seated at a desk or workbench, or even
while walking. It is a brief, practical prayer that relates the
concerns of everyday life to the ever available power of His com-
panioning Presence. It is a habit which takes prayer out of the
ivory tower and relates it to the real concerns of life. If there
have been failures in attitude, if there have been moments of
irritability, if there has been any un-Christlikeness, here, while
it is all too freshly stamped upon our consciousness, we bring
our confession to Almighty God and ask the cleansing of His re-
newing grace. Or again, we have been in contact with someone
who needs the Presence of God, or we have seen someone else
who has grown tense amid the burdens of his work; and now,
in this moment of quiet, we offer up a brief prayer of intercession on his behalf. Or still again, it may be that the throngs
of people among whom we move quicken our consciousness of

the larger concerns of God's Kingdom among men, and our intercession reaches out with fresh vitality, asking God's guidance for community or state or nation. The more regularly we observe this brief noontide pause, the more real will be the interplay of prayer and life; and this one disciplined moment will lead to many other spontaneous acts of devotion amid the pulsing currents of actual life. Again and again, throughout every day, we will find ourselves offering brief prayers, uttering religious ejaculations, calling upon God, until His Presence becomes for us a continuous experience.

d. Vesper Devotions. At the close of the afternoon, before concern for the evening meal crowds in upon her, the woman in the home might well observe her vesper tryst with God. On the other hand, a man coming to his home before the dinner hour might habitually plan a few moments of Bible reading and prayer in this pause at the end of his day. Still others might find it better to go apart for their vesper talk with God after the evening meal. Thanksgiving is a natural part of such a prayer, for surely each of us can find many evidences of God's grace for which to raise a prayer of gratitude at the end of the day. Here, too, belong confession and the offering of new resolutions that can become creative on the morrow. In this prayer, also, there should be a large place for intercession as we lift those nearest and dearest to us into the light of His Presence. Our devotional Bible reading should frequently be our preparation for the prayer of meditation which may become central in our devotions the next morning. In all ages the spiritual instinct of man has led him to walk and talk with God in the closing hours of the day.

e. Evening Prayer. If our waking thoughts belong to God, so also do our final moments of consciousness before we go to sleep. This is not the time for our longer prayers and devotions. We are too sleepy, and our energy is too spent. This good-night prayer should be a very simple one in which we quietly, peacefully, and confidently entrust our souls to the care and keeping of the Almighty Father before we rest in the stillness of refreshing sleep. This is not the time for facing problems nor for our highest spiritual concentration; it is rather the opportunity for realizing the deep wonder of God's eternal care for each of us, His love-begotten children.

These five prayer periods should be established as a minimum rule for our personal devotions. They are separate from our practices of family prayer and the saying of grace at meals. While they may be adapted to suit our needs as individuals, they should not be departed from lightly, for they have grown out of the practice of the masters of the spiritual life through the ages. There is sound wisdom and psychological effectiveness in such a program. If we were to neglect many of the suggestions in this book but resolved to embark upon a new life of prayer simply by keeping these five prayer periods as a sacred and binding covenant between ourselves and our God, we should go far toward that spiritual renaissance for which we are seeking. If, on the other hand, we were to read books upon books concerning prayer and yet not have the integrity of devotion to practice faithfully some such rule, we should find ourselves achieving a deceptive familiarity with techniques and vocabularies about prayer, but we should have lost its reality and power. Our spiritual growth waits upon our moral decisiveness and our realistic discipline.

Many of us will want to go beyond this suggested rule of prayer. In talking with E. Stanley Jones about prayer, I once asked him concerning his practice. He told me that in India he had more opportunity for extended periods of prayer.

"While in America I have to pray by the clock," he added. "I set apart a half hour in the morning, a half hour in the middle of the day, and a half hour at night for prayer. If I do not do this, I notice the difference—not in the long run, but right away."

The setting apart of longer periods of prayer has been characteristic of all powerful spiritual leaders. John Wesley used to write each year in the forefront of his journal: "I resolve 'Deo Juvante'—1. To devote (to retirement and private prayer) an hour morning and evening—no pretense or excuse whatsoever."

45

How well he knew our human frailties is shown in that final phrase, "no pretense or excuse whatsoever." Francis Asbury habitually arose at four or five o'clock in the morning and gave from three to four hours to study and prayer, and before retiring for the night gave at least one hour to like pursuits. The flames that burned in the soul of Martin Luther were kindled in the place of prayer, where he felt that he must spend not less than three hours in any day. Most of us doubtless are not ready for such extended periods of prayer. But it is significant that the men of greatest power have always been souls disciplined by the might of prayer. Surely, however, every Christian is called to begin the life of devotion by establishing and maintaining his own unvarying rule and habit for spiritual devotion.

CHAPTER IV

The Training Ground of the Spirit

DISCIPLINE—IN LIFE

Study to show thyself approved unto God, a workman that
needeth not to be ashamed, rightly dividing the word of truth.
—II Tim. 2:15

WHILE OUR MISSIONARIES WERE STILL IN CHINA, ONE OF THEM
was striding along the top of a section of the Great Wall. He
overtook a young Chinese man, and as they talked together, the
youth asked him why he was walking so briskly. The missionary, who had been a star fullback, answered, "I am in training."

"For what game are you getting in condition?" the youth
asked.

"The game of life!" was the answer.

Everyone knows that you cannot win games or break records unless you are in condition. We sometimes have overlooked the parallel fact that we cannot achieve spiritual heights
unless we have trained and disciplined our lives.

1. THE DISCIPLINE OF SOLITUDE

Places to pray are not easy to find in the modern world.
It takes concentrated effort to establish a sanctuary of solitude
where we may be alone for prayer.

The world is too much with us; late and soon,
Getting and spending, we lay waste our powers.[1]

[1] William Wordsworth, untitled sonnet.

We are always in a tumult of voices; we are always being jostled by other people; we are immersed in noise and confusion. And the worst of it all is that there is no place where we can get alone to repossess our souls. Years ago Edward Bok had carved above the mantel in his home: "I come here to find myself; it is so easy to get lost in the world." We must, then, through disciplined effort establish places for private prayer.

Most of us today live in crowded apartments, and even when we have the luxury of a private room, we are self-conscious about going away from the family group for prayer. Yet how much more we should have to contribute to our families, or the group with whom we live, if there were available places where we could rally and steady our spirits in God's Presence. The first step for those of us who live in homes might be to call a family council where without embarrassment we might plan together times of solitude for each member of the family. After all, the only way to meet problems in life is to face them squarely, and we may find that the whole atmosphere of the home will be changed if one member has the courage to raise this question and make the worship of the Heavenly Father natural for each one. Young couples planning marriage might well talk this matter over together as one of the sacred preparations for their new home.

In one home where this was discussed a husband and wife planned that during the evening they would make it their natural practice for each to spend a little time in the uninterrupted privacy of a special room where he could have his individual vesper devotions. In another home a wife arranged that her husband should have time for his morning devotions while she prepared the breakfast. Then, after the family had left, she planned a devotional period for herself to begin at twenty minutes of nine, so that without considering the clock she might hear it strike the hour and know that the planned part of the period was ended. Parents could render their children a real service by talking this matter over with them and then having it understood that there would be times of privacy which would be respected for each of the children. It would do much to steady youth today if they had such a haven of quietness in their homes. Like every problem of life, there is only one thing to be done: face it. The solution will be found much more easily than we feared.

If we make up our minds to achieve a sanctuary for prayer, all of us can do so. The vice-president of one of the largest corporations in America told me how he took a part of his noon hour alone behind the locked door of his conference room for his major period of devotion. A young woman working as a technician in a hospital laboratory found that she could have access to the laboratory room alone during the noon hour. Many people find in chapels or sanctuaries of churches an impersonal place where they may pray undisturbed. Every church should seek to establish the custom of making its sanctuary an available House of Prayer for all people.

Whatever our solution may be, reality in prayer depends upon the discovery of a place where the soul can relax in the knowledge that during the period of prayer we will be undisturbed. Whittier used to go to a Friends Meeting House for his devotions. Concerning it he wrote:

> And so I find it well to come
> For deeper rest to this still room,
> For here the habit of the soul
> Feels less the outer world's control;
>
> . . . .
>
> And from the silence multiplied
> By these still forms on either side,
> The world that time and sense has known
> Falls off and leaves us God alone.[2]

2. THE DISCIPLINE OF ENRICHMENT

The richness of our prayer life depends upon what we bring to it. In every other realm we know that our knowledge and

[2] "The Meeting."

interest condition our enjoyment and appreciation. A symphony concert means more to us if we have some understanding of its background. Pierre and Marie Curie came with unflagging zest to the dirt, inconvenience, and unattractiveness of their laboratory because of the immense profundity of the knowledge of physics which they brought into the room with them. They moved with mastery in the realm of the physical elements, seeking the elusive secret of the mystery of radium. How drab, empty, and meaningless that laboratory would have been to the average, untrained person! The principle applies everywhere. Mention your favorite hobby to some uninterested friend and notice his blank or bored expression. If perchance you know nothing about law, go into a lawyer's office and observe how little interest you have in the problems which he finds so absorbing. It is the background that we bring to any experience that transforms it from empty meaninglessness to rich attractiveness.

For all too many Christians the experience of prayer is as a symphony concert to the musically unawakened, a laboratory to the uninstructed, a hobby to the uninitiated, or any realm of business to the inexperienced. One of the disciplines which we need in prayer is such an enrichment of our spiritual background as shall bring us to our devotional experience with quickened zest and awakened interest.

No preparation for prayer can ever excel a growing and deepening acquaintance with the Bible. For all too many people the Bible is like an unknown city. We open its pages and feel like foreigners. Its streets and avenues bear unfamiliar names like Ecclesiastes and Thessalonians. Its houses seem closed and forbidding. If we try to locate the address of some indistinctly remembered friends, the names and verses through which we search are as impersonal as a telephone directory. Have you ever observed, however, what a change can come over an unfamiliar city when you move into it? By degrees you make new friends. Faces come alive for you, and people become warm and human. The doors of houses open, inviting you to the friendships within. The halls and churches and shrines become centers of living inspiration. By degrees it becomes your city; you feel at home; you belong. Even so should our experience be with the Book of Books. Here are the pathways to the City of God; here are the records of great pioneers of the spirit; here are kindling insights and stimulating experiences; here are great revelations of God and His dealings with mankind; here walks the Master who can guide us into the very Presence of the Eternal; here moves the Presence of the Holy Spirit. An acquaintance with such a Book is primary for prayer.

What is needed at the place of prayer is a devotional approach to the Bible. We must learn to "read the Bible biblically." God's Word still speaks. Under the living influence of the Holy Spirit words can come alive in our experience and insights can flame into illuminating visions as we devoutly sit in the presence of these inspired messages. It is the living reality of God breaking through into human hearts and speaking His kindling and creative words which we seek.

But first we must become familiar with the physical setting of Bible events. If we will read in a Bible atlas about the Holy Land; look at pictures of costumes, houses, and scenery; relate the geographical features of lake and limestone hill, seashore and plain, to countryside with which we are familiar, we need not read the Bible against an unvarying backdrop of neutral gray. We will be able to see its colors in birds and flowers, Oriental garments and glowing faces, sungleams on Galilee and starlight over Bethlehem, deep ravines filled with purple shadows and barren deserts drenched with glaring light. We will hear its sounds in night breezes through cypress trees, in storm winds over dashing lake waters, in children's laughter and women's voices, in men excited in the market place and quieted in prayer, in raindrops on flat roofs and thunder rolling over tall mountains. We can then enter into the lives of its characters as people who lived like us—human, with quick anger and abiding love, with hopes and thwart-ings, with dreams and disappointments, with boredom and ecstasy, with depression and deliverance. In a word, we can re-create it in our mind through study and bring it to life through imagination.

Whatever our method of Bible study may be, we need to set apart some period each week to deepen our acquaintance with the Word of God. Then as we pick it up in some moment of preparation for prayer, we will find its deathless words speaking with clearer meaning to quicken our mind and spirit for adventure into the Presence of God. Central in the sanctuary of prayer for all Christians is the Word of God. No other preparation can fully replace its use. Nowhere else can we find stimulus so available and so real as here. The only way to restore the Bible to its lost primacy in our American life today is by its rediscovery as the supreme Book of the inner life by thousands of everyday Christians in every city and hamlet in our land. When its majestic words come to life for us, a new era of spiritual discovery will have begun.

In addition to the Bible there are many other sources of enrichment available for all who would develop a growing life of devotion. Our hymnals can become a treasure house of devotional materials, particularly if we will take time to memorize some of the more inspiring verses of loved hymns. The reading of books of prayers and familiarity with the great devotional classics of the ages could not but add new depth to our spiritual appreciations.

3. THE DISCIPLINE OF A RULE OF LIFE

But what is called for ultimately, if we are to advance in a pilgrimage from self to God in the life of prayer, is a far more fundamental discipline of all of life. We accomplish this by adopting for ourselves a carefully considered rule of life. It will seem strange at first to undertake this type of planned and controlled existence, but there is no way to mastery in the spiritual life except through some such practice. Our rule should include the following three emphases:

a. A Rule of Prayer. Against the background of what has been said in these chapters we should now write out for ourselves, or determine, the definite rule of prayer which we are willing to establish through a sincere covenant with God. From time to time in high moments of consecration we may desire to revise and extend the rule which we have adopted. Surely we shall want to check up, in our time of self-examination, to see how faithfully we have kept our promise to God. Many of the suggestions to be presented in the following chapters will point toward a regulated life of prayer. By this path alone can we arrive at greater freedom and power in the spiritual life. Spontaneous prayer will always have a place in our life, and an important one, but the difficulty is that for so many of us prayer is more haphazard than spontaneous. It needs direction by a consecrated Christian will. This is a holy thing to which we are now summoned. On our response a great part of our spiritual destiny may hinge.

b. A Rule for Daily Living. If we are to achieve the heights of practicing the Presence of God, we must begin to live now in the knowledge that He is near us every moment. We are therefore called to adjust every part of our daily lives to His will and to adopt definite rules for making all our actions more Christlike. We proceed to work out standards for being more Christian in our chosen vocation. We adventure in the Christian control of money through a program of tithing and stewardship. We decide upon certain advances to be made in our home and in our relations with people. We map out procedures for our growth through devotional and other reading. We determine where Christ wants us to serve Him, perhaps in some humble way. Let us not begin with too many rules. Let us keep it all very simple. Let us keep it joyous and flexible by avoiding scrupulosity, and sincere and determined by overcoming laxity. It is all a happy adventure entered upon by our free choice. We have awakened to a new awareness of God's Living Presence. Let us make this vital new religious insight a controlling force in our daily lives.

c. A Rule for Christian Growth. The transforming of our lives, and ultimately of the very citadel of our being, is essential if we are to make progress on the upward way that leads to communion with God. Human pride is the root of most of our failures. Self-love does more to destroy our peace and to disturb us than almost anything else. Over against these, what we now need is a sense of our dependence on God's upholding power, an awakening in our hearts of love for God, and an increasing surrender of our wills to His control. We are called to adopt a rule of practical next steps for our Christian growth. We must simplify our lives, relieving them of their complexity by relating them to their one center, God. "Thou shalt love the Lord thy God with all thy heart, and with all thy soul, and with all thy strength, and with all thy mind." (Luke 10:27.) We must detach ourselves from domination by possessions and things. It is amazing what release will come when we realize of what secondary importance many possessions are. We must work to achieve true humility. We must seek to be delivered from dependence upon the desire for human approval. "Study to show thyself approved unto God." We must strive to practice self-control, patience, and self-denial. To enable us to do this we must follow a few simple rules concerning the Christian virtues which we desire especially to cultivate. It is always better to aim positively at a virtue to be practiced than at a fault to be overcome. It is much more interesting to try to acquire something than merely to avoid something. Included in these rules for our Christian growth must be a commitment to regularity of Christian worship at our church, together with participation in acts of Christian dedication and service.

Further suggestions for self-examination and self-discipline will be given later, after we have learned the methods of meditation, but now at the very beginning we must make our start, recognizing that Christlike living must accompany Christian praying at every point. How better could we grow as

Christians than through the adjustment of life to God's will through some practical and definite life plan?

4. THE DISCIPLINE OF METHOD

Finally, we need to venture with new methods of prayer, training ourselves in various forms of vocal and mental prayer and ultimately coming to the experience of contemplative prayer. Spontaneity in the use of our familiar ways of praying must never be lost, but we must not shrink from the effort involved in disciplining our spirit to new ways of making prayer real. What pioneers of the spirit have found valuable in all ages can bring to our lives contributions of inestimable value.

We have awakened to the reality of God; we are questing His Presence. No price in terms of training and discipline is too great if thereby we are enabled to meet our God face to face.

PART TWO

Contact with Power

CHAPTER V

How God Answers Prayer

PETITION

If ye abide in me, and my words abide in you, ye shall ask what ye will, and it shall be done unto you.   —John 15:7

"THERE WERE OTHER HANDS THAN MINE ON THOSE OARS." These were the words spoken by James C. Whittaker at the climax of that grueling experience of the men on the raft after their plane had plunged into the Pacific. We all recall this incident vividly from the newspaper accounts if not from reading his book *We Thought We Heard the Angels Sing.*[1]

Weakened by twenty-one days of practical starvation and merciless exposure, Whittaker and two other members of the crew were overjoyed at the sight of a distant island. Whittaker got out the aluminum oars and, summoning his last reserves of strength, began to propel the rubber boat toward the little coral atoll whose palms bore the promise of water, coconut milk, sustenance, life. Aided by the current that had borne them thus far and his terrific exertions at the oars, they were making it. He could see the palm trees clearly, together with the waves breaking on the sandy beach. They were almost to safety when suddenly the current shifted and, in a matter of moments, whirled them more than a mile out to sea. With its relentless grip it would sweep them past the island to more days of drifting, hunger, thirst, and pitiless burning of the tropic sun, more than flesh could long endure.

[1] New York: E. P. Dutton & Co., 1943.

Then Whittaker prayed. Earlier they had all discovered a strange power in prayer. Now in his supreme extremity—defeated by this coalition of natural forces, beaten down into elemental dependence upon a Power greater than himself—he prayed. The muscles of his arms were little more than flabby skin over bone. Almost the last vestiges of his energy had already been expended. But then he prayed and, having prayed, grasped the oars again. Desperately he pulled for that passing shore. Somehow there was new-found strength in his rowing, but the terrible undertow of the current still held the raft. He tugged on the oars till one of them bent from the pressure. Then he saw that he was gaining. Yard by yard he fought his way against the current until finally he swept into the peace of the inner lagoon, and in a little while the boat grounded on the rough coral sand of the shore. Life, food, friendly hands to help, safety! Looking back he said, "There were other hands than mine on those oars."

Were there? If it is true that prayer brought power in this extreme circumstance, as Whittaker so devoutly believed, then may not prayer be of dynamic help to everyone? This is the problem that rises from the yearning hearts of men everywhere. Does prayer in any real sense bring us into contact with the power of God?

1. AN ELEMENTAL AND UNIVERSAL EXPERIENCE

Through all ages and in all places, the testimony of mankind is that something happens to release power when men pray. The very survival of this form of prayer bears testimony to something here of far more than superficial meaning. The testimony of the centuries is too widespread to be ignored by any scientist of the soul who is searching for spiritual facts. Prayer as the soul's cry to God in every extremity is so instinctive that we cannot avoid the experience. We may have rationalized. We may have felt that the modern world has outgrown prayer as petition. But when the great emergency comes to any one of us, we pray. We cannot help it. As Sabatier said,

"Man is incurably religious." When the crisis strips him bare of customary ideas and the pose of sophistication—in the hour of stark need—man cannot avoid praying.

Under the terrifying stress of modern war a whole generation of youth have prayed in this way. Those cries flung Godward in the dark crises of battle still trouble us. They were so arresting and real in their intensity that we cannot lightly brush them aside. Caught in the grip of tragic forces, men were impelled by an irresistible urge to cry out for help to whatever Power there is in the universe. We cannot think of God turning aside from such prayer merely because it does not move upon the highest level of Christian experience. He in whose heart is everlasting Fatherhood surely responds to such sincere, and often agonizing, prayer.

But it must at once be admitted that much of this prayer is on the primitive level. It is real and elemental, but it is frequently not developed and mature. Those who embark upon the adventure of high Christian prayer should aim to grow toward as completely developed and focused an experience as possible. What is needed in this realm, then, is not so much new techniques—since this experience springs so spontaneously out of the deep needs of our lives—but rather as clear an understanding as possible of the foundations that underlie prayer as petition.

2. THE FAITH ON WHICH PETITION RESTS

No matter how man may have become enamored with the descriptions of our universe by science, basically he knows that he, as a conscious personality striving for values, is a product of the Universe. He, too, is an incontestable fact produced by the vast Process. He cannot regard himself as a cosmic accident. Man, though limited and conscious of his human weakness, never loses his confidence that he is in some way akin to God. He never escapes from the persisting belief that all the power of the universe is controlled by a sovereign purpose, and that God the Creator is also Conscious Personality. It is a return to this basic assurance that comes in crisis hours. It is an inescapable conviction of meaning and rationality in the whole scheme of things that drives a man to make his final appeal to the Almighty. Prayer in this sense is the very essence of religion. It is man desperately breaking through everything that hinders him with the dynamic assertion: "I believe in God the Father Almighty. He made me. He cares for me. He has power adequate for my needs."

3. THE NATURE OF CHRISTIAN PETITION

But now we must face the nature of our contact with the power of God through prayer. Prayer is the process of lifting life up into alignment with the will of God. It does not consist in the assertion of our will. It does not demand that every wish we utter shall be fulfilled. Prayer is not magic. It is not rubbing an Aladdin's lamp to bring the quick fulfillment of every vagrant desire. We would not really want to live in such a universe. Which of us would dare to substitute our limited, blind, imperfect—often sinful—wishes for the will of the Almighty Father? We would not want to live in a universe so capricious and so undependable. Surely no human wish should occupy the ultimate throne of the universe. It is just because we need a wisdom and a power greater than our own that we cry out in prayer. We truly want God's will to be done. In our humanity and our helplessness we want Him to take hold of a baffling or threatening situation and lead us through. Prayer is the means whereby we bring life into attunement with the powerful purposes of God.

Jesus, the great Master of prayer, did not promise that God would answer every request that we make. The heart of His teaching on this aspect of prayer is found in His promise: "If ye abide in me, and my words abide in you, ye shall ask what ye will, and it shall be done unto you." (John 15:7.) He promises clearly that prayers will bring contact with the answering power of God, but this divine response is conditioned by the very nature of prayer itself. God's powerful will is moving forward, actuated by His omniscience, His holiness, and His love. In prayer we lift our lives up into oneness with the eternal purposes of God. We abide in His Presence. We are molded in accordance with His word.

Prayer has its conditioning laws which are as real in the realm of the spirit as the laws of physics are in the realm of electricity. In this latter realm man discovers that as he truly adjusts to the innate nature of electrical energy he can make contact with the onflowing stream of its forces. He releases their power to the extent that he really understands them and effectively co-operates with them. In prayer we adjust our humanness to the level of God's great intentions for us and through us. Successively, step by step, we rise till our lives are flowing along in the direction of His almighty will. Whenever this is achieved, we are at the place of power. We have reached a contact point from which some God-intended results will follow.

A DIAGRAM OF PETITION

The onflowing will of God

Contact with God's power

Communion with God

Lifting our wills to God's will through the adjustment of prayer

The answering response of God in our life situation

Our egocentric desires

4. HOW PRAYER IS ANSWERED

God can answer prayer in various ways. He is not limited merely to the realm of the dramatic and the miraculous.

a. Through the Release of Power Within Us. The enhancement of our own strength and the releasing of resources latent within us is one of these ways. We are surcharged with new energy with which to face life's pressing demands, or we are guided to new insights of ways in which we can proceed.

Recently in talking with a group of high school boys I said to one of them: "Suppose that you come to a life situation where you are an x quantity facing a $2x$ situation. How could God solve this life equation as you prayed?"

"He could reduce the $2x$ situation which was too big for me to handle so that it would be only x," he replied instantly. There was a momentary pause, and then he added, "Or He could make me a $2x$ person."

This is what happened in an incident which Pearl Buck has given us out of the life of her mother. On one occasion this mother, a missionary in China, found herself alone with her children and a maid "when she received warning that a band of rough men was coming one night to kill them all. She went by herself and prayed, 'If it be Thy will, save us, but in any case, help me not to be afraid,' then knelt for a long time thinking what she must do, and rose, with a plan in her mind which she bravely carried out, a plan which saved them all." [2] She would not have been equal to the situation without prayer. Prayer is a very real factor in helping us to quell our panic, release our latent powers, reinforce our thinking, and open our souls to God's creative action. Prayer makes us channels through which the divine power can flow to transform the situation into one of triumph.

b. Through the Co-operation of Others. The lives of men and women offer another channel by which God answers our prayers. They too are the instruments for the accomplishment of His will. We pray for health. It may be that some

[2] *We Can Pray* (Cincinnati: Forward Movement Commission), p. 39.

wise doctor has through years of discipline caught glimpses of the laws of God at work in the human body. It may be that God will guide us to him as the instrument of His healing will. Or again, we pray for rescue, and God's impulse of mercy finds fulfillment in an aviator winging over the ocean in ceaseless search for our drifting raft. We are all bound together in the bundle of life, and God is depending upon our co-operation to achieve many of His purposed goals. Sometimes as we wait for an answer to prayer, we should feel the sacredness of an approaching person as if he were in fact the instrument of God's answer.

> Hush, I pray you! .
> What if this friend happened to be—God? [3]

c. Through Direct Creative Action. The most direct way in which prayer is answered comes when the creative will of God is brought powerfully to bear upon some situation. We must believe that God is free to answer our prayers.

While we recognize the insights of science and accept all the truth which scientists have, through patient research, been able to establish, we nevertheless place the systems of science in the total frame of reference of a Christian philosophy which refuses to make God a prisoner in His own universe. He who created all things, who is the World Ground of unity and harmony and rationality which is assumed by all science, is limited only by His reason, His righteousness, and His love. God is capable of self-direction. In the total scheme of things one of the most significant aspects, surely, is purpose—the power of God moving toward the achievement of worthy goals. The freedom of the Divine is not restricted to the great underlying structures of His universe; it is operative in the particulars as well. There is room in the world for God's present, creative action at any point which does not conflict with His wisdom, His holy will, or His spiritual relation to His free

[3] Robert Browning, "Fears and Scruples."

children. God can answer all prayers that do not conflict with these essentials of His eternal nature.

But, someone objects, it is just because the Eternal Reason has established natural laws that we cannot expect prayer to be answered. We do not want to live in an arbitrary and unpredictable universe. Its regularity and dependability spring from the Omniscience that established these laws. There is a large measure of truth in this objection, but it is not ultimate. A mature Christian would not expect God lightly to set aside the normal processes which He has ordained. But he realizes that natural law is only a name for the regular way in which God does things. There is no natural law apart from God. There are not two controlling powers in our universe: the one, God, and the other, natural law. There is no conflicting dualism at the heart of things. There is only one ultimate controlling power—God the Father Almighty.

The universe is open and not closed. We know that the moral nature of God and the spiritual purposes of God are more significant aspects of reality even than His creative power in nature, for it is in these great areas of divine action that the meaning of the total process is to be sought. In any situation, then, these realities of divine action should always be expected to be present, and they are the decisive and controlling factors in the complex of forces operative at any given moment.

The universe exists for personality, and for the production and conservation of values in and through persons. It exists for the fulfillment of the highest purposes of God. If these purposes can be better fulfilled and these values more perfectly achieved through an emergently creative newness of divine action, we must assume that God is free to act in this way. He never violates His natural laws. He rather lifts the regular ongoing process up into the operation of still higher expressions of divine energy. It is impossible for Him to do an irrational thing that violates the order of His universe, but He can transcend the orderly processes of the physicochemical level in obedience to the higher laws of His essential Being, such as the laws of divine purpose, will-to-value, and love of persons.

If we consider just one of the natural laws alone, something may be impossible, but it is possible for the intelligence of man so to combine laws that he can accomplish purposes which might at first seem impossible.

For instance, in 1903 Professor William North Rice sat at his desk on the campus of Wesleyan University and wrote: "I do not believe that any man in this age and nation—at least any man of sound mind and education—can pray that . . . a heavy body which is left unsupported may be poised in air above our heads." [4] Yet, even as he was writing his argument for the impossibility of God's answering such a petition, the Wright brothers were tinkering with a machine in which, before the year was over, they were to fly through the air at Kitty Hawk. And a few years ago when I flew over the campus where Professor Rice wrote his book, the students scarcely bothered to look up at the heavy body unsupported in air above their heads. Man had not violated any natural laws to achieve this result which only half a century ago was accounted impossible. He had merely utilized the interplay of a higher complexity of laws to achieve his purpose of flying. He had caught the law of gravity up into the more complex frame of reference of the laws of aerodynamics. What man can thus do, why should we think the Almighty cannot do?

A radio broadcasting set on a ship at sea is a purely mechanical device controlled by absolute laws of physics and electricity. And yet its very existence is designed to serve purposes of mankind. In the hour of emergency it flings its SOS out through the storm to summon help. No physical law has been violated. It has been used for the rescue of human lives.

We must not blink the facts which modern science has revealed. We must face every real fact. Otherwise there will always be a lurking fear that prayer is just some psychological projection of our desires against the impersonal swirl of atoms

[4] *Christian Faith in an Age of Science* (New York: George H. Doran, 1903).

that constitutes the real universe. Men cannot pray powerfully while nagged by self-conscious doubts. Only the harmony of clearest thought with deepest instinctive outcry can give poise and confidence in emergency hours. Fearlessly facing all facts, we must hammer out a vital faith and, on the basis of this, recapture the assurance that man does receive power through prayer. The impelling force behind all things is the rational, loving, value-creating purpose of God. There are undoubtedly times when man's co-operation with God in prayer fulfills the moral and spiritual conditions for the release of His emergent purpose.

5. WHEN PRAYER IS NOT ANSWERED, WHAT THEN?

We have said that no scientist of the spirit can overlook the continually recurring, widespread, ageless fact of answers to prayer. On the other hand, we must not turn aside from the hard fact that some prayers are not answered as we wish.

a. An Ultimate Rather than Immediate Answer. In some of these cases a longer-range view would reveal that a deeper answer is being worked out according to some more ultimate purpose of God. Sometimes our prayers are too importunate. In our humanness we cry for immediate answers. "Now," we cry, "give me deliverance! Now, in this way, answer my prayer!" Paul has pointed out that it is the whole pattern of life which reveals how things work together for good to those who are in the will of God. Sometimes we need God to sustain us in patience while waiting for an answer not yet come. It may be that He is preparing to answer the dominant desire of our hearts rather than the form of our present request.

In one of the most impressive passages in his "Confessions," St. Augustine pictures his mother, Monica, praying all one night, in a sea-side chapel on the north African coast, that God would not let her son sail for Italy. She wanted Augustine to be a Christian. She could not endure losing him from her influence. If under her care, he still was far from being Christ's, what would he be in Italy, home of licentiousness and splendor, of manifold and alluring temptations? And even while she prayed there passionately for her son's retention at home, he sailed, by the grace of God, for Italy, where, persuaded by Ambrose, he became a Christian in the very place from which his mother's prayers would have kept him. The form of her petition was denied; the substance of her desire was granted. As St. Augustine himself puts it: "Thou, in the depth of thy counsels, hearing the main point of her desire, regardedst not what she *then asked,* that thou mightest make me what she *ever desired.*" [5]

Often our limited life span on earth will not be long enough for the working out of the fulfillment of God's eternal purposes. To us who believe that eternal life begins now as a new quality of our experience of God and of the life that results from communion with Him, the larger meanings of our existence are still ahead. Often in our darkest hours we must in prayer rise to the high faith which was in the heart of Christ when He said, "Father, into thy hands I commend my spirit." (Luke 23:46.) Easter vindicated His faith. Christians believe that eternity will likewise bring to us God's ultimate answer to every good prayer of the human heart.

Mothers whose boys prayed in the foxholes of war but who were not saved from the bullet's mark have then this ultimate consolation—that in very fact all things work together for good when the entire pattern of the love of God shall one day be unfolded in the realm of immortal life.

b. The Answer in the Experience of God's Presence. Here is another way in which we may approach the problem of unanswered prayer. We may recognize that the real answer to all prayer comes through a more vital personal experience of the Presence of God. True prayer is God-centered. Our supreme objective is to commune with Him. His love is so strong and abiding, His power so completely equal to His purposes, His Presence so near and so unfailing, that we can trust Him utterly. Our quest is attained when we enter His Presence. The true answer to prayer is the experience of God by our side. This was the unexpected answer that came to Paul in the

---

[5] Harry Emerson Fosdick, *The Meaning of Prayer* (New York: Association Press, 1934) , p. 125. Used by permission of the publishers.

crisis of his life. Here was one of the greatest Christian leaders who ever lived. Suddenly he found himself handicapped by the unceasing throb of a thorn in his flesh. What was it— dimming eyesight, crippling arthritis, or some malady that suddenly struck him down? No one knows. But it was evidently some affliction that was harder than all the other sufferings that the great apostle had been called to endure. Three times he went to his knees, crying out to God again, and again, and again, that it might be removed; but still the aching handicap remained. Here so often we stop praying. We cry out that prayer is a failure, that God has not answered us. But Paul was made of sterner stuff. He kept right on praying until at length he said, "God answered me." But it was not the answer which he had expected. Though unexpected, it was a very real response to his cry. "And he said unto me, My grace is sufficient for thee." (II Cor. 12:9.) Suddenly Paul felt the gracious love of an understanding Companion close by his side. He sensed a sufficiency that made him able to bear whatever might come. He now knew that in the hardest hour he could rest back upon a Power that would see him through. He realized the personal emphasis of the words "for thee": God was interested in his problem, knew all about his burden. He, as an individual, was very precious in God's sight. Out of this experience Paul was able later to say, "I can do all things through Christ which strengtheneth me." (Phil. 4:13.)

All prayer is answered. The answer is the experience of God Himself, sometimes manifested through the release of new energies within us, sometimes revealed through the action of God's other children who come to our aid, sometimes released in the change of the situation itself through God's creative action upon it, sometimes unveiled in the ultimate answer which He is unfolding, and sometimes discovered in a new consciousness of His powerful Presence by our side.

In the face of the ultimate mystery of suffering we pose no simple answer to the problem of the tragic element in human existence, but we find in prayer deep contact with One who has shared our suffering. One evening in the circle of an intimate group of ministers and laymen in Chicago, Dean Charles W. Gilkey of the University of Chicago was opening his heart to share the deep faith which he had hammered out face to face with life's sternest problems. What he then said adds one further note to the values which lie in the heart of prayer.

It makes a very great difference at this critical point when you can bring these tragic experiences into the presence of the cross of Christ. I thought in my youth that the cross was chiefly a symbol of what damage the stupidity and sin of men can do. In later years it has come to mean much to me to realize that it is also a symbol of the eternal mystery of suffering and evil in a tragic world where God's ways are not as even Jesus wished or thought or prayed— witness Gethsemane. These matters pass beyond our human understanding and keeping, also, into the care and keeping of God. There are some profound words of Dora Greenwell that I discovered as a student at Oxford in 1910; I have been learning ever since what a difference they can make in the presence of suffering.

"The deeper these thoughts sank within me, the more complete became my dissatisfaction with the shallow theories through which human thinkers have striven to bridge over contradictions which God has left unreconciled, and to reply to questions which He has been pleased to leave unanswered. That death of anguish which Scripture declares to us to be 'necessary,' though it does not explain wherein its dire necessity resides, convinced me that God was not content to throw, as moralists and theologians can do so easily, the whole weight and accountability of sin and suffering upon man, but was willing, if this burden might not as yet be removed, to share it with His poor, finite, heavily burdened creatures. When I looked upon my agonized and dying God, and turned from that world-appealing sight, Christ crucified for us, to look upon life's most perplexed and sorrowful contradictions, I was not met as in intercourse with my fellowmen by the cold platitudes that fall so lightly from the lips of those whose hearts have never known one real pang, nor whose lives one crushing blow. I was not told that all things were ordered for the best, nor assured that the overwhelming disparities of life were but apparent, but I was met from eyes and brow of Him who was indeed acquainted with grief, by a look of solemn recognition, such as may pass between friends who have endured between them some strange and secret sorrow, *and are through it united in a bond that cannot be broken.*"

So is it finally in the presence of the mystery and the tragedy of death: for death is tragic as well as mysterious to those who love— especially early death. The familiar arguments pro and con about immortality convince few of us and comfort fewer. What Christian faith gives us here is not argument, but history and experience: this early death that looked utterly tragic at the moment but proved afterward to be powerfully redemptive; and most of all, an experience of life with God through faith in Christ, which it is convinced the death of the body cannot interrupt nor destroy. "For I am persuaded, that neither death, nor life, . . . nor things present, nor things to come . . . shall be able to separate us from the love of God, which is in Christ Jesus our Lord." [6]

This is the ultimate answer to all prayer: a deep, real, and unshakable experience of the Presence of the eternal, Christ-hearted God, with us always. He is never nearer than when, in life's tragic hours, we need Him most. Then He comes in answer to our prayers with understanding love and sustaining power; so say all who, "being in an agony," have cried out in the hour of their midnight anguish for the help of God.

The prayer of petition takes its place for a mature Christian in the totality of the prayer experience. It is never cheap, superficial, selfish, or aggressive. As our consciousness of God deepens, our confidence increases. To the extent that our contact with Him is strongly made, new powers are released through us and new creative actions of God are initiated. As we grow in the life of prayer, our petitions will be concerned more and more with supplication for the spiritual gifts and graces of which all souls stand so constantly in need.

There is one further problem to be faced: Is human prayer needed when God is all-knowing and all-loving? This will be discussed in the next chapter in connection with that specialized form of petition called intercession, wherein our requests are raised to God for others.

[6] Charles Gilkey, "Apologia," unpublished manuscript. Used by permission.

CHAPTER VI

For Their Sakes

INTERCESSION

I pray for them. . . . And for their sakes I consecrate myself.
—John 17:9, 19 A.S.V. mg.

> More things are wrought by prayer
> Than this world dreams of. Wherefore, let thy voice
> Rise like a fountain for me night and day.
> For what are men better than sheep or goats
> That nourish a blind life within the brain,
> If, knowing God, they lift not hands of prayer
> Both for themselves and those who call them friend?
> For so the whole round earth is every way
> Bound by gold chains about the feet of God.[1]

Do we share this faith of Tennyson? Do we believe that prayer changes things? Do we believe that something really happens when we pray for other people? When someone we love is in danger, or is suffering, or is facing a hard hour, does prayer for that person really help? Does it make any difference when we pray for peace to return to the earth, or for God's Kingdom to come in some needy area? Do prayers for people and for great causes really change things?

Jesus believed that they did. He Himself constantly was praying for other people. When He came into the presence of a man who was deaf or dumb or blind, He would lift His eyes to heaven and pray for him until His intercession was answered

---

[1] Alfred Tennyson, *Idylls of the King*, "The Passing of Arthur."

and the healing power of God was made available. He prayed for Peter, asking that his loyalty might not entirely fail and that his life might not be shattered. In His high-priestly prayer in the Upper Room He prayed for His disciples, saying, "I pray for them. . . . And for their sakes I consecrate myself." On the cross He prayed for the multitude that was putting Him to death, crying out: "Father, forgive them." Even there He felt that the prayer of intercession could be significant for God and could so influence the events that these people might be forgiven.

You and I pray like that when we are off guard, when we are not inhibited by a too critical spirit. Strong souls who deeply love cannot avoid praying for others. It may not matter so much to them what they endure personally, but the heartbreak of others wrings from them a quick cry for God to help those whom they love. If you have a little child who is desperately ill, you cry out to whatever Power there is in the universe, saying: "O God, help this child!" To pray for those whom we love is the very essence of both love and prayer. The greater the stature of a person, the wider is the outreach of his prayer for others.

Whatever problems may be connected with intercessory prayer, the fact of its universal, elemental, and instinctive nature points to the conclusion that there is something real here. But the problems must be frankly faced.

What happens when we pray for others? Does it do any good? How can my prayer really affect another person's life? Even if it could, would it be right to abridge another person's freedom and exert this influence upon him? Why should another's destiny depend upon my spiritual action? Why should we need to prompt a God of love and wisdom to do something good for another person? These are real questions raised by sincere people, and it is such questioning that has in modern times cut the nerve of prayer for others. If they are not faced, our instinctive outcry will be hesitant and partly inhibited. We are dealing here with a pivotal question in making prayer real.

1. PRAYER CHANGES THE PERSON WHO PRAYS

When one person prays for another, the first result is that the one who prays is changed—that is, provided he prays. There is no magic in saying certain formal words addressed to Deity. But whenever anyone prays, something tremendous takes place. Perhaps we can picture it by a triangle. At one point is the person who is praying. From this point we draw a horizontal line to the second point, the person prayed for. Then we complete the triangle with a line from each point up to the apex, which is God.

If our praying remains merely our human concern for another, merely the expression in words of our desires for the other person, it is horizontal prayer and moves only along the base line on the earth plane.

But what if instead we reach up and attune our life to the Infinite, link up with the intentions of God, really pray? Prayer means communion with God. Prayer means some degree of oneness with God. If in any way in the reality of our worship we become deeply conscious of God, then we are praying. So the first thing we do is not move out on the horizontal line, not cry out superficially, "God bless that person," but rather take time to be sure we are lifting ourselves up into an awareness of the Divine, that we are linking ourselves with God—in a word, that we are praying.

As we do this, subtle but unmistakable changes are taking place in us. From the apex of this established communion in the presence of God we now see the other person as God sees him. When we do a thing as powerful and tremendous as that, there are consequences in our own life. When we really become aware of the living God, when reality comes to us in prayer, then we are changed.

We can no longer be selfish, egotistical, and self-centered. The relation of the other person to us is no longer subjective. It is so often terribly true that our relation to others revolves around our interest in ourselves. Other persons are merely adjuncts of our ego. Sometimes we react against people. Sometimes when they are boorish, crude, or ignorant we say, "You can't do this to me," emphasizing the personal pronoun "me." Prayer delivers us from these subjective reactions. We begin to see the other person as Christ sees him. No matter how disagreeable or sinful the person may be, Christ yearns over him with an everlasting pity. We begin to see life through the other person's eyes. We put ourselves in his place and begin to ask, not, "What does he do?" but, "Why does he do it?" We begin to see intuitively into that tangled maze of thwarting and frustration that has produced his aggressive behavior, to see the redemption that could come if God's will could be fulfilled in him. No matter what he has done, he is still a child of God, and round about him is God's unyielding love. We begin to glimpse the real problem: "What could God do to release this soul?"

Again, when we are praying for someone whom we love in a time of crisis or terrific need, prayer changes us. We are delivered from our fear and our agitation. We simply cannot stay in the realm of the available love and power of God without realizing what God could do for that person.

Sometimes, on the other hand, we are not concerned about the people for whom we should feel a concern. If we pray until we begin to sense the purposes of God for the redemption and benefit of all mankind through Jesus as revealed on the Cross, we cannot ever again be entirely indifferent to other people. We are sensitized to a new way of looking at people. Their concerns are not something foreign to us. They are not "another race of mortals bound on other journeys"; they are our brothers and sisters. We are kindled and made ready for Kingdom action. We are made ready to do what we can. We somehow stimulate others to a conspiracy of friendship that helps lift loads from human hearts.

We are transformed when we really pray. The first thing to do in intercession, then, is to pray until we adjust ourselves to God's will, condition ourselves to God's Presence, and awaken to the tremendous reality of God in Himself. That is the first thing—we must really pray. As we become conscious of what

God's presence means to us, suddenly it dawns upon us that the supreme thing that could happen to others would be a similar entrance into the place of God's Presence. We cry out for God's Spirit to enter their lives, for His power to be manifested to them, for His love to enfold them, and for His will to be done in them. We are concerned not merely to busy ourselves in superficial actions, but to strive with God for abiding solutions to the problems which they face.

2. PRAYER INFLUENCES THE OTHER PERSON

Many people would be willing to acknowledge that prayer changes the person who prays, but they stop there, thinking that the only value of prayer is a subjective one. For them it is merely a more or less valuable form of autosuggestion. But there is a basic insincerity in praying for another person if all that we expect to happen is that we will be changed. Why not then just limit our prayers to ourselves? There is a certain hypocrisy in saying, "God help that person," unless we really believe that something is going to happen at the other end. We all tend to shy away from psychological techniques whose only objective is to lift ourselves by our own bootstraps. Only when we are convinced that it is influencing the other person can we pray with wholeheartedness, sincerity, and the drive of deep earnestness.

But you say: How is this possible? How can we interfere with the life of another person? Should not that person's freedom be respected? Is he not an autonomous individual in his own right? Yes, he is. But that is not the only rule of life. There is the principle that a man is free, that ultimately he cannot be coerced by another; but there is a second principle, namely, that he can be powerfully influenced by another. In every realm this is so. Did you ever stop to think of the influences of evil that are playing upon people's lives? Of the tragic influence of war upon many lives? Of the pressure that is exerted upon a person who happens to live in the slums?

For good or evil we are bound together in the bundle of life.

The fact of social solidarity implicates us in the consequences of others' sins, or grants us the gracious heritage of other men's achievements. War does lay its brutal tragedy on all of us. Slums do clutch at the souls condemned to live in them. Moral evil corrupts and contaminates the lives of those it touches. Degrading social conditions powerfully influence every life. While salvation is ultimately an individual affair between a man and his God, on the other hand many obstacles to his redemption could be removed if the Kingdom of God came in the social culture in which man is immersed.

Every individual who lives in accordance with God's will helps to change the atmosphere of society. The intensity and power of one's experience of Christ releases a healing stream to flow into the life of society. How great is the influence of a Christian parent! How strong the leadership of a dedicated prophet! How kindling the influence of a Christian teacher! How wide the outreach of heroic altruism in a Jane Addams or an Albert Schweitzer! Such personalities are like the opening of windows through which sunshine and fresh air may stream into the infected atmosphere that others breathe. Every man is influencing others daily. The whole course of our lives contributes to the blessing or cursing of mankind. It is not to be wondered at, then, that when we pray, and thus rise to the very highest action of which we are capable, our social influence can become enormously powerful. One of the greatest influences in life is exerted when some noble and consecrated person prays for his fellow men.

If we know that someone is thus praying for us, this is undoubted. If some true friend sincerely says, "As you go into the valley of your suffering, I shall be praying for you," there comes an inevitable uplift to our spirit. On the other hand, many of us have had the experience of standing beside some soul in the shadows of life and having him turn to us and, out of the depth of his anguished need, say quietly, "Do not forget to pray for me." In life's crowded hours of suffering or tragedy the value of the prayers of others is strongly underlined.

One day Jesus, earth's greatest man of prayer, was walking along a dusty road among the tramping throngs. He felt the nervous touch of a woman who reached out to grasp his mantle in the hope that something of His healing power might be available for her. "And straightway Jesus, perceiving in himself that the power proceeding from him had gone forth, turned him about in the crowd, and said, Who touched my garments?" (Mark 5:30 A.S.V.) If we, like Him, could be transformed by the consciousness of the Father's presence and indwelt by the spirit of God's love, our prayers for others would make us to become radiating centers of spiritual healing and power in the lives of those who touched our garments day by day.

Reginald J. Campbell, one-time minister of City Temple, London, passes on a record of the tremendous spiritual influence exerted in the life of the distinguished missionary John G. Paton by his father:

That father was a stocking weaver, a poor man in one of the poor districts of Scotland. "But," says J. G. Paton, "he was a man of prayer." There was one little room in between the "but" and the "ben" of that house, as the Scots call it, into which he retired daily, and often many times a day, "and," says the son, "we children got to understand by a sort of spiritual instinct, for the thing was too sacred to be talked about, that prayers were being poured out there for us as though by the high priest within the veil of the Holy of Holies. We occasionally heard the pathetic echoes of the trembling voice pleading as if for life, and we children learned to slip out and in, past that door on tiptoe, and not to disturb the holy converse. The outside world might not know, but we knew whence came that happy life, that new-born smile that was always dawning in my father's face. It was a reflection from the divine Presence in the consciousness of which he lived. Never in temple or cathedral of mountain or glen can I hope to feel that the Lord God is more near, more visibly walking and talking with men than under that humble cottage roof of thatch and open work. Though everything else in religion were by some unthinkable catastrophe to be swept out of my memory or blotted from my understanding, my soul would wander back to those early scenes and shut itself up again in that sanctuary, and hearing still the echo of those cries to God, would hurl back at doubt with the victorious appeal, 'He walked with God; why may not I?'" [2]

There is no short cut to influence like this. A deep spirit of intercessory prayer, a sincere love for others, a creative awareness of God's power and willingness to help all His children— these are the necessary conditions of spiritual influence. Prayer for others influences them through the spiritual quality which it begets in the man who prays.

It is not difficult for us to grasp the fact of spiritual influence upon those who touch our garments, but can intercessory prayer bridge gulfs of distance and still produce results in the life of one prayed for? Certainly this is true if we know that someone is praying for us. No distance can prevent the impact of a strong soul upon us when we are aware of his love and spiritual concern. But what if we neither touch the garment of the person who prays for us nor know about it? Does prayer still help then? We must believe that it does. But for the discovery of the source of this intangible but real power we must move out of the realm of personal influence on others into the central sphere where the praying soul communicates with the Father Heart of God, and where a new situation arises with a creative significance that springs from our real contact with the Presence of God.

3. INTERCESSION IS SIGNIFICANT FOR GOD

Prayer not merely changes and transfigures the one who prays; prayer not merely influences the other person; but, if it is real prayer and the powerful spiritual fact that it should be, prayer for others is also significant even for Almighty God. But you say: How can this be? If God is good, and if God is love, does He not will the best for each person? In His great wisdom does He not will the finest possible solutions? He does not need any prompting from me, does He?

---

[2] *The Song of Ages* (New York: A. C. Armstrong & Son, 1905), pp. 106-7.

One of the finest answers that I have seen to this objection is voiced by Bernard Clements, who says:

It is true that God wills to do what is best for every human being, but it is also true that over and over again He wills to do it through you and me. If when you go out presently you come across a man hitting a little girl on the head with a brick, I think you will feel quite certain it is God's will that this should be stopped, and if you are the nearest person handy you will be tolerably sure that the stopping of it should be done by you. You do not just lean in a nonchalant sort of way against a wall and say: "It's perfectly all right. God wills what is best for the little girl, anyway, so I needn't do anything in the matter." You get into the middle of things at once and stop it, even if you get hit on the head yourself in the process. Well, in very much the same way, God wills the best for the various cases of need about which from time to time we become aware, and over and over again He wills that that best should be brought to those cases by the spiritual strength and refreshment of which our prayers can be the channel.[3]

One of the reasons why the Kingdom of God does not come faster is that there are not enough people sensitized to the Spirit of Christ through prayer, not enough people who are open channels through which God's will can come.

When we pray for another, a new spiritual fact is created which God desires but which did not exist until we prayed. Our prayer, then, is a significant reality even for God. It is not that God in His love for others needs human prompting to manifest His holy will. His dream of the highest good for each of His children is as constant as the love from which it ceaselessly proceeds. But God is moral and is eternally limited by His own righteous nature, through which He continually respects the freedom of the children whom He has created. God never coerces human beings. There is at the center of our universe no dictator who forces us to acquiesce in his purpose. God's will

[3] *When Ye Pray* (London: Student Christian Movement Press, 1937), p. 39. Used by permission.

and His Kingdom wait for the free and willing co-operation of spiritually autonomous persons.

Whenever there arises a deep spiritual response, in prayer, of creature to Creator, of man to his God, then God's highest intention finds fulfillment. A new spiritual fact emerges in the universe, which God has long and anxiously awaited. In the high laboratory of human character God awaits the result of His greatest experiment. Or like an eternal Gardener He awaits the opening of the perfect lily which He has long struggled to produce. Or, most deeply of all, like a human father He yearns for that moment when a choice youth stands up in the midst of temptation to reveal the strength of character which flames into being in some crisis hour. So God awaits the emergence of the supreme spiritual fact: a man who shares his redemptive spirit and rises to the height of a soul who truly prays for another. This is the summit of creation for which God has waited long.

Here God's creative intention for some one of His children finds a new spiritual instrument through which it can work. God could not create this open channel until some soul rose to the high fulfillment of his potential spirithood. God's will is being held back constantly because not enough such channels are open for His power. His pledge of love is constant and un-changing. He yearns to bless and help His children. But the medium through which this help can be released is the opened heart of a responsive soul. Anywhere that a soul responds to God, God can come in. The person prayed for may not as yet have opened his heart. God does not batter down the door. He exerts every spiritual and moral pressure for our good, but ulti-mately He waits for our response. When another responds for us, it means that some approach to our nature is possible. There is a deep and abiding truth in the vicarious law whereby an-other can stand in our place, and through the open channel of another life God's influence can find a new opening through which to play in blessedness upon our soul. In prayer some lonely child of the spirit pioneers in the laboratory of com-munion with the Eternal. He comes into oneness with God's purpose of love for mankind, and releases the divine intention through the spiritual reality of his prayer.

When we pray for others, we are fulfilling the will of God; when we do not, we are blocking the will of God. Every person is spiritually a channel or a barrier. The Kingdom of God has not come more quickly upon the earth because there are not enough channels open through the lives of those who really care. So often our prayers have been narrow and limited; we have only prayed for those nearest and dearest to ourselves. We can measure any personality by the amount of time he spends in intercessory prayer. If we want to know whether or not we are growing spiritually, we have but to consider how much time we have spent this past week in praying for people everywhere. In order that we may grow in our outreach, why not set apart one day each week to pray for our friends and our families; a second in which to pray for particular people who are especially in need of the sustaining help of God; a third in which to pray for people whom we know who are not active followers of Christ; a fourth in which to pray for our local church and for the Church universal; a fifth in which to pray for our missionaries and the peoples of other lands; a sixth in which to pray for our own community, its youth, its underprivileged, and its leaders; and a seventh in which to pray for our nation and its leaders, and then for all nations and for their blessing through the coming of peace, justice, freedom, and good will to all the earth? Some such program of regular prayer would inevitably develop in us a wider outreach, a deeper sympathy, and a more vigorous life of intercessory prayer.

While it is true that the intercessor is thus the channel of God's grace, we still must consider the nature of the power which is made available when a sincere Christian prays. Recent scientific studies of telepathy have revealed that the psychological influence of one person on another, even at a distance, is an inescapable fact. This is not an adequate interpretation, however, of the dynamic of intercessory prayer. It does suggest the possibility of a force that can operate from one heart to another when we pray. God has established all things and upholds them ceaselessly. He has created this psychological mechanism, and is free to use it to wing our prayers to influence another soul. But it is not an ultimate nor an adequate description of the supreme power which is available in intercession. We are not limited to mere telepathy in itself, nor to any vague help out on the psychological periphery of extrasensory perception.

Nor, again, do we find an adequate explanation in the collective unconscious. We cannot accept any doctrine of a corporate soul that ultimately abridges the autonomy of the free individual. We do not go back in intercessory prayer to some hidden power welling up from the unconscious depths of the racial inheritance we bear within us. Rather do we rise to the sublimation of that raw energy in a Christian social consciousness whose basic nature is love. Our psychological pilgrimage is, as Fritz Künkel has pointed out, from the "I" to the "We" to the "He." [4] The individual should take his place in a group vitally participating in the larger life of mankind. But human brotherhood depends ultimately upon the Divine Fatherhood. The individual achieves his highest selfhood when he awakens to his relationship to the Creator who is at work in his group relationships. We therefore conclude that the ultimate account of the power available in intercessory prayer is not to be found in the descriptions of psychological processes. They can indicate that direct influence of personality upon personality, as in telepathy, is an accepted fact. They can further call to our attention that we are all more deeply interconnected than we realize. For the real dynamic, however, we must turn to the realm of religion.

There is in the individual what has been called "the fine point of the soul." It is the home of the spiritual capacity of man to enter into communion and contact with the Spirit of God who indwells him. When we pray we are not merely putting forth human energy. We have achieved a state of spiritual communion with God. God is active in the process. "Like-

---

[4] *In Search of Maturity* (New York: Charles Scribner's Sons, 1943).

wise the Spirit also helpeth our infirmities: for we know not what we should pray for as we ought: but *the Spirit itself maketh intercession for us*." (Rom. 8:26.) In intercession we are working with God, and God is working with us.

If God is calling men to co-operate with Him in the work of establishing His Kingdom, may we not also believe that God is calling men to co-operate in the supreme work of the Eternal, to enter into spiritual oneness with that "great love which like a fire is ever burning in His heart"? This in deepest reality is what we mean by intercession. We are participating in the love of God. We are uniting our wills with that of the loving Father. In the ground of our souls we have entered into kinship with the indwelling Holy Spirit. We have been privileged to co-operate with God in His almighty work in the souls of men. The Holy Spirit of God dwells in every person. It is in the measure of oneness which we establish with the indwelling Spirit through prayer that we are brought into union with and influence upon one another.

Someone might ask: But why, if God is thus the ultimate medium of influence in our prayers, are we needed at all? No analogy is adequate to express this fact. Perhaps a suggestion from Leonard Hodgson comes as close to the reality as any:

We may perhaps think of our prayer as the kindling and fanning of a spark within us. The spark is a spark from God's eternal flame, and itself grows into a flame, one with that flame of God which is the source of all light and warmth. Those for whom we pray are warmed and lighted by it, and in them, too, the spark is kindled and springs up into flame.[5]

How God uses our prayer for others we may not know, but that He does we are powerfully assured by the final realities of our faith.

The redemptive outreach of God is not blocked ultimately if we fail to pray. Mankind failed Him supremely at Calvary. By

[5] *Concerning Prayer* (London: Macmillan & Co., Ltd., 1921), p. 229.

the greatness of the action of His redemptive passion He transcended their rejection. The Almighty can make the wrath of men to praise Him. Eternally He initiates fresh and powerful approaches to the human heart. But while we cannot by our lukewarmness and indifference in prayer and intercession ultimately defeat the will of God, we can tragically delay the coming of His Kingdom. When Jesus taught us to pray, "Thy Kingdom come," He revealed that man has a part in the responsibility for the achievement of God's purposes of love for mankind.

The greatest force in the world is the power of God. When we open the doors through our prayers, God's power will stream in, and results beyond anything we have expected will take place. We are not fully Christian until once again there is a mighty revival of intercessory prayer in the conviction that it is one of the greatest powers in all the world. May God help us to take our stand by the side of the praying Christ in the Upper Room, as with Him we quietly say: "I pray for them. . . . And for their sakes I consecrate myself."

PART THREE

The Way of Spiritual Discipline

CHAPTER VII

The Pilgrimage from Self to God

PATHWAYS OF PRAYER

And the Lord called Moses up to the top of the mount and Moses went up.   —Exod. 19:20

THE TOTAL LIFE OF PRAYER IS LIKE A CLIMB UP A MOUNTAIN. Many people are content to dwell on the plain or to immerse themselves in the bustle of the city and never to make the effort of really mounting up into the very Presence of God. They know that the eternal summit is always there, looming up mysteriously in the distance against the horizon. They believe in its existence; they count upon it as one of the landmarks of their lives. Sometimes they stand in awe and appreciation of its distant beauty. But they never feel impelled to leave the city of man and start out upon the trail that leads to the higher vantage points of prayer. There are multitudes, however, who do hear the call and start up the slopes in quest of the heights.

Emily Herman has defined prayer as "the pilgrimage from self to God." [1] As we have started out upon this trail, we have already seen that there comes a moment of awakening in which the heights become real and strangely relevant to our lives. We have caught a glimpse of the shining white glory of the majestic summit which we now desire to scale.

One day we start out upon the ascent. We begin to condition ourselves by hiking over the foothills and the frontal ranges. We know that the journey will be long, and we carry large packs for our comfort on the way.

[1] *Creative Prayer,* p. vii.

89

The first stage of the trail is through the forest that covers the lower slopes. It leads uphill but is not too demanding. It is easy to follow, for it is a well-worn path over which many feet have passed. There are also blazes on the trees and other guide-posts which we can follow. We now catch at intervals more intimate glimpses of the peak, but it is partly obscured by the surrounding trees.

After we have camped and journeyed and gone on for a considerable time, we find that the landscape is changing. The trees are thinning out and becoming dwarfed. We have reached the timber line. Now a new climb is before us. It is over broken boulders, granite ledges, and high ridges. The way is more open. We are freed from the narrow path; we can see the general slopes and choose our own trail. There is a strange mingling of the quietness of great solitude and the invigoration of bracing atmosphere. In the shelter of glacial ravines among the cliffs there are mountain tarns beside whose still waters the exquisite flowers of the uplands are blooming. Here we may rest in quiet and beauty. The peak is now gloriously near. As we surmount each rocky ridge, we see it towering before us. Sometimes the clouds are about it. Then, as they break away, it appears again, so near as to be breathtaking, as we glimpse the awesome mystery looming right above us.

And now at long last we come to the final demanding heights. We have reached the snow line and are out upon the eternal glaciers. Before us there is a towering cliff that appears to block our way, but there is no other path to the summit. We have now left our packs behind us and are stripped of every excess weight. Tremendous winds roar about us; and then the clouds rush in, surround us, and obscure our pathway. All the beauty has disappeared. Finally, as we struggle up the dangerous precipice, night engulfs us. The climb demands all there is in us, but at last we master its ultimate test. The light returns, the clouds billow about us, and then we break out into the clear above them. The sun is rising, and the mists are shot through with the rose light of dawn. They roll back like mighty curtains to reveal the vision of a transfigured world. We are struck speechless by the radiance that suddenly dazzles our eyes as we front the inexpressible glory of the summit.

No figure of speech can accurately portray the journey of the soul on its high pilgrimage of prayer; but, if you will not press it too far, this does suggest the larger aspects of the way on which we have now started. Multitudes through the centuries have climbed the trail. Some have tried to analyze their experience and name and describe the regions through which they passed. Thus there has developed a system of classic terminology by which to designate the various stages and forms of prayer. Most writers on the higher levels of prayer use these classic terms. One who seeks to grow in prayer should therefore get acquainted with them.

The lower forest-clad slope, where we train and condition ourselves as we climb, has been called classically the Purgative Way. Using a designation for this stage more familiar to our generation, we shall call it the Way of Spiritual Discipline.

The more open ledges above timber line, where glimpses of the summit are more frequent and more intimate, are known as the Illuminative Way, or, as we shall phrase it, the Way of Illumination.

The final demanding heights have for centuries been referred to as the Unitive Way. We shall use the name the Way of Oneness with God.

There are certain forms of prayer and devotion that are characteristic of these three stages. Before we continue along these spiritual ways, let us pause to chart and define the total journey.

1. TRAIL GUIDE FOR THE PILGRIMAGE

Within each of the three ways of our pilgrimage there are classic forms of prayer, worship, and devotion. In living expression prayer does not stay fixed within any diagram. It is a spontaneous, free, and direct fellowship of man with the Eternal. Nevertheless, there is a high degree of validity in this analysis which comes from the rich devotional experience of the ages.

a. The Way of Spiritual Discipline

1) *Awakening,* in which, as we have already discovered, an experience of the reality of the Divine Presence kindles our souls with a desire to start upon the higher road of prayer.

2) *Vocal Prayer.* This does not mean prayer spoken out loud, but rather prayer in which words are the predominant feature. Examples are a ritual prayer such as the Lord's Prayer, or a conversational prayer, frequently referred to as a "colloquy." Vocal prayer may be quite formal, or it may be lifted, as will be suggested, to the level of high worship. An unusually effective form on this higher level will be presented under the name "act of devotion."

Petition and intercession, which we have just considered, are also forms of conversational prayer. They have been treated separately because they are originally a spontaneous form that is primitive and elemental. They spring from the psychological root of prayer, a consciousness of a felt need by the individual or by him on behalf of his group. They rise, however, to higher levels and recur in more developed forms as we advance in prayer.

3) *Meditation.* This is a brooding prayer in which we reflect upon and try to make our own some spiritual truth. It is also called "mental prayer," emphasizing the part that reason and thought play in this experience. Still another name which is sometimes used for this same form is "discursive prayer." This name does not mean that it is a rambling prayer, but rather— getting back to the root meaning of the word—that it is a discourse, as in consecutive and logical thinking. Any consideration of an attribute of God, an event in the life of Christ, or a passage of scripture, in a reflective and prayerful mood, is a meditation.

Meditation is the most effective method of prayer for "purgation"—the process of purifying our hearts, disciplining our actions, adjusting our wills to the will o... our lives into conformity with the life of our... seek to apprehend the will of God and the mi... our lives. Then, in the awareness of God's holy... seek through self-examination, confession, forg... and resolution to grow in grace. Psalm 51 is typical of the spirit of the prayer of meditative purgation. Mental prayer of this nature is frequently called a "spiritual exercise."

At its highest, meditation involves not merely thought but a free outpouring of the feelings of our heart toward God— somewhat in the mood, for example, of Psalms 8 and 150, but more intimately. Such meditation is known as "affective prayer," or the Prayer of the Heart, and is considered a transition between meditation and the next higher stage.

b. The Way of Illumination

Contemplation is the usual name for the form of prayer in this part of our pilgrimage, referring to the focusing of our consciousness on God. It is a freer and more direct form of communion. Its loving outreach toward the Divine culminates in a real, personal awareness of His Presence. The word "illumination" in the name of this way of prayer refers to God's gracious action in illumining our hearts and minds through the radiance of His Presence.

Classically three stages of contemplation (sometimes referred to as "degrees of orison") have been distinguished: the Prayer of Simplicity, in which we simply and lovingly turn our attention toward God and pray freely, intimately, and directly; the Prayer of Quiet, in which in deep stillness we wait receptively for God's coming; the Prayer of Active Contemplation, in which we experience briefly the illimitable wonder of the actual touch of God upon our lives as we contemplate the immediateness of His Presence. Through the ages there has also been recognized, implicitly in practice, a fourth stage, in which we share the passion of Christ—the vicarious love of God—and are led to a supreme spiritual response in devotion to His will and cern for His Kingdom. We may make this explicit as the fourth stage of contemplation, calling it the Prayer of Vicariousness.

The term "active contemplation" is sometimes used to describe all these stages of contemplation rather than the third stage alone. This is done to emphasize the fact that, while God by His action brings to us the illumination of His Presence, we are still active in co-operating with Him as we come to this exalted experience. It is therefore a normal and possible privilege for every vital Christian. It seems better, however, to restrict this term, as is done here, to the single stage of the Prayer of Active Contemplation, which it precisely describes, and to use the general term "contemplation" to cover in a broad way all four stages.

c. The Way of Oneness with God

Most of us will enjoy the prayer of contemplation which has just been defined. Some of us may feel God calling us to a still more intimate oneness of spirit with Him. As we advance to this supreme height, we are aware that we are being led by the Spirit of God. He is entering, or being infused, into our very heart. This is so characteristic that this highest stage of the life of devotion is sometimes called "infused contemplation." It is a truly mystical experience in which God is acting directly within the depths of our souls.

Our highest oneness with God demands the total surrender of ourselves. The ultimate struggle with our pride, our self-love, and our self-will is tremendous; and while we are engaged in it, our attention is diverted from the joys and spiritual consolations that have previously made our way radiant. For this reason John of the Cross, who first analyzed the experience in detail, gave the stage of final surrender the descriptive name by which it has been known for four centuries, the Dark Night of the Soul.

When we have, through this preparatory experience, been brought into living oneness with God, then we discern that the darkness has been but the prelude to the final joyous harmony of our lives with God, which is called the Transforming Union.

2. CLARIFYING THE TRAIL SIGNS

Along the trail of Christian prayer which we are seeking to climb there are certain trail signs the meaning of which we should come to understand before we proceed.

a. Prayer, Worship, and Devotion. These three terms are so interblended in meaning that they cannot be fully defined except in relation to each other. This is because they are all concerned with the very essence of religion—our living relationship with God, conceived as real, personal, and present. In prayer we come into relation with God through communion, contact, and interaction; in worship through reverence, homage, and adoration; in devotion through love, fervor, and consecration. When we do not pray, we break the vital link that unites us with God. When we do not worship, we cut ourselves off from the supreme worth and eternal value which is at the heart of the universe. When we do not practice the life of devotion, we lose those supreme motivations which alone give meaning, significance, and purpose to our existence.

Worship and devotion find their truest and most essential expression in prayer. Prayer is lifted to its highest levels through worshipful awareness and adoration, and through devoted surrender to the will of God and consecrated concern for the coming of His Kingdom. Thus we see how these three terms, while each standing for an essential emphasis, really so overlap that they cannot be permanently separated. They are inherent parts of the very essence of religion itself. The experiences which they denote flow into, supplement, and complete one another. They unite in all our most profound experiences of the Eternal.

b. Prayer and Mysticism. "Mysticism" is a classical word which stands for a definable Christian experience at the high point of our religion. This experience has nothing to do with the vague, occult, abnormal, and sub-Christian experiences of pseudomysticism. Again, it is only remotely related to the non-Christian mysticism of the Orient, which Friedrich Heiler defines as "that form of intercourse with God in which the world and self are absolutely denied, in which human personality is dissolved, disappears and is absorbed in the infinite unity of the Godhead." [2]

Over against this we have from Evelyn Underhill, a leading Anglican writer in this field, the following definition of essentially Christian mysticism:

Mysticism, then, is not an opinion: it is is not a philosophy. It has nothing in common with the pursuit of occult knowledge. On the one hand it is not merely the power of contemplating Eternity: on the other, it is not to be identified with any kind of religious queerness. It is the name of that organic process which involves the perfect consummation of the Love of God: the achievement here and now of the immortal heritage of man. Or, if you like it better—for this means exactly the same thing—it is the art of establishing his conscious relation with the Absolute.[3]

Miss Underhill would call the entire pilgrimage of prayer which is presented here The Mystic Way. This does not mean that she regards every stage of it as mysticism, but that the whole process leads up to our increasing and ever-deepening oneness with God which is at its climax a mystic experience.

If we think of the term "mysticism" in a general sense as meaning any real awareness of the Divine, it is immediately apparent that prayer is of this nature. However, in its fully developed form we do not come to a truly mystical experience until we reach the highest stages of prayer. A. Poulain, one of the oustanding authorities in this field, states: "We apply the word 'mystic' to those supernatural acts or states which our own industry is powerless to produce, even in a low degree, even momentarily." [4]

[2] *Prayer*, p. 136.
[3] *Mysticism*, p. 81. Used by permission.
[4] *The Graces of Interior Prayer* (St. Louis: B. Herder Book Co., 1950), p. 1.

Let us adhere to this more precise usage. There are grounds for distinguishing mystical elements in the higher stages of contemplation, but we may reserve the term "mysticism" in its fullness to denote those forms of extraordinary prayer which will be discussed in the last two chapters. All the rest of the book is concerned with God's gracious action within the soul in ordinary prayer which should be the normal experience and the high privilege of every real Christian.

Concerning the higher states of mysticism it should be pointed out that they may more properly be called supernormal than abnormal. While it is true that there has been a fringe of abnormal experience associated with the lives of some mystics, this is not the normative element, and it is always deprecated by the great mystics themselves. The saints of the ages who trod the higher reaches of the spirit were men and women of heroic mold. They were personalities who were tremendously effective and powerfully influential.

Most of us, I greatly fear, will not be troubled by mysticism. Its moral demands are too great, its rigorous exactions too costly, and its high disciplines of the human mind, heart, and will too terrific for most of us to achieve. But the very knowledge that these heights are there, and that some of the greatest pioneers of the spirit have reached them, calls us on to a life of continuous development and never-ending advance. In the life of devotion there is always more beyond. If we have advanced a little distance on the road, we shall be saved from spiritual pride by the knowledge of how far short we have come of the ultimate experience available to devout followers on the higher road that leads to the Transforming Union of our lives in contact with the Presence of the Eternal God.

3. THE PILGRIM WHO CLIMBS THE TRAIL

Having surveyed the various stages of our pilgrimage from self to God, and having made clear to ourselves the meaning of the major trail signs which we shall meet along the way, we now turn our attention to the pilgrim himself. When he uses these various forms of prayer, what is happening within his soul? What are the major spiritual impulses that actuate him on his climb?

He is advancing steadily toward the high peak of oneness with God. This is his one aim, and this gives unity to the process. We can analyze this into *four dynamic spiritual movements toward God* which are going on in his soul. They are:

a. Stillness, a turning from the surface self to the God-intended self.

b. Recollection, a turning from self-centeredness to God-centeredness.

c. Awareness, a turning from self-consciousness to God-consciousness.

d. Response, a turning from self-will to God's will, and from self-love to God's love.

At every stage of our pilgrimage along the three ways of prayer and in the use of the various forms of prayer we shall observe these dynamic soul movements toward God taking place within us. At first, as we are disciplining our lives by climbing over the foothills and frontal ranges, they will appear as techniques, willed attitudes, and intentional actions. God is calling and leading us to them, but they must be initiated by our effort. As we move on toward the timber line in the higher developments of vocal prayer and meditation and in the earlier stages of contemplation, we shall discern an increasing interaction of God's will and our wills in these four movements of our souls toward Him. As we approach the peak itself in the higher stages of contemplation and as we mount toward the Way of Oneness with God, we shall observe that increasingly the divine action predominates in these processes.

The four major spiritual movements can be analyzed most clearly into their separateness at the start of our journey. They draw together into unity as we approach our goal of oneness with God. There they are clearly seen as but four emphases of the one essential process of prayer, the soul's pilgrimage from self to God.

We shall then see how the process of stillness leads us from our surface selves to our deep selves, where we begin to be aware of our kinship with the personality of God. This merges imperceptibly into recollection, where we are turning from our self-centeredness and increasingly centering ourselves on God. This experience in turn flows into the experience of awareness, in which through our deepening God-consciousness we are being led to contact and interaction with His Presence. And finally, as the consciousness of God over against our lives dawns upon us, we instinctively sense the divine demand to adjust our lives to His in an act of response. These are the essential movements of religion itself. Through them prayer is lifted up to the heights of its fulfillment as worship and devotion.

One other thing should be observed concerning this process within our souls as pilgrims on the climb to God. We now come to see that our progress up the mountain has not been along a straight, upward-sloping path, but rather along a series of switchbacks that zigzag up the mountain. Again and again we come to the same major ridges and ravines on ever higher levels.

The techniques of relaxation and willed stillness with which we begin in vocal prayer mount up progressively to higher forms of this experience in the second stage of contemplation, the Prayer of Quiet. Our preliminary recollection is enriched through the God-centered forms of prayer in meditation until in the contemplative Prayer of Simplicity our whole souls are through loving attention concentrated on God. Awareness begins in the moment of our awakening, continues through our deliberate affirmations of faith, deepens through the enrichment of our convictions in mental prayer, and rises to the mysterious moment of illumination when we are led by His Spirit to the immediate Presence of the living God in the Prayer of Active Contemplation. Response begins the moment we come into any contact with God, even the most elementary. In conversion our response may be profound and soul-changing. As we awaken to the Living Presence of God and hear Him calling us to come up higher in our spiritual lives, we respond by purging away our grosser sins and seeking to conquer our other sins and imperfections. As we grow in grace and pass from the Way of Spiritual Discipline to the Way of Illumination, this same spiritual movement continues, only now on the higher level of contemplation. Our lives are now being simplified from their complex struggles with particular failings, and we are moving more positively to center our whole soul in a loving response to God. We are seeking simply and directly to imitate Christ in our lives. We are striving to change from self-will to God's will at the center of our being. At the same time we are nearing the completion of another part of our total response to God, the change from self-love to God's love. The call to consecration and devotion has been sensed in the earliest stages of our pilgrimage. As we have come into more real communion with God, this positive phase of our response has become ever more central. As we advance toward the height of contemplation, we find ourselves sharing ever more profoundly the experience of God's living love with which we are in prayerful contact. In the Prayer of Vicariousness we come to sense our interaction with the eternal love that constitutes the very heart of God.

All of these Godward movements of the soul continue on even higher levels as we rise toward the summit of possible spiritual experience in mystic communion, contact, and interaction with God, the Transforming Union.

Now that we have mapped out the entire trail ahead, made clear the meanings of our major guideposts, and analyzed the spiritual motivations within our souls, we are ready for the climb ahead.

CHAPTER VIII

Transforming Our Everyday Prayers

VOCAL PRAYER—DYNAMICS

But thou, when thou prayest, enter into thy closet, and when thou hast shut thy door, pray to thy Father which is in secret; and thy Father which seeth in secret shall reward thee openly.

—Matt. 6:6

ONE NIGHT SOME YEARS AGO I CAME INTO MY STUDY BURDENED with a sense of discouragement and defeat. The stock market had crashed; the economic foundations of our country had been shaken; and our church was in the midst of trying to pay off the mortgage on its new building. This night in our board meeting we had faced apparent failure. Yet somehow it had seemed to all of us that this undertaking was God's will for us then. I threw myself upon my knees and began to pour out my heart in earnest words for God to help us in our crisis. But when I had said Amen, I began to realize how nervous and disturbed I had been as I prayed, how much my attention had been absorbed in my problem, and how little I had been aware of God. It was prayer, all right, and the gracious God whose ear is always open to the sincere cry of His children had heard it, I knew; but it did not move upon the higher levels of prayer as worship.

I turned off the light in my study and stepped to the window. For some time I stood there looking out at the quiet serenity of the eternal stars against the blue velvet background of the sky. Gradually peace returned to my heart. Then I snapped on the light, seated myself at my study table, and turned the pages of the Bible until I found myself reading the tremendous assurances in the fortieth chapter of Isaiah: "Hast thou not known? hast thou not heard, that the everlasting God, the Lord, the Creator of the ends of the earth, fainteth not, neither is weary? there is no searching of his understanding. He giveth power to the faint; and to them that have no might he increaseth strength. . . . They that wait upon the Lord shall renew their strength." (Isa. 40:28-31.)

Then I went once more to my knees in prayer. What was the first word which I uttered this time? Absolutely nothing. I just grew still and waited in the quiet sense of His nearness. Then slowly and thoughtfully I repeated the well-known Collect for Purity of Heart:

Almighty God, unto whom all hearts are open, all desires known, and from whom no secrets are hid; cleanse the thoughts of our hearts by the inspiration of Thy Holy Spirit, that we may perfectly love Thee, and worthily magnify Thy Holy Name; through Christ our Lord. Amen.

The words "Almighty God" began to glow in my thoughts. For several minutes I meditated upon them, blending the strong words of the Scripture with the thoughts and memories that these words evoked. And now I saw my problem transfigured. If God's almighty power willed it, this task could be accomplished. It was no longer my burden alone. There were two of us to share it, and the great Other was God. I had but to dedicate myself to His purposes and humbly ask to become a channel, poised and ready to give everything of which I was capable, but ultimately dependent upon His almightiness as the source of real power, to achieve our goal.

And I smiled to think God's greatness flowed around our
    incompleteness,—
        Round our restlessness, His rest.[1]

[1] Elizabeth Barrett Browning, "The Rhyme of the Duchess May."

Parenthetically, He did lead us to the accomplishment of our goal, and in ways so marvelous that none doubted they were of His leading. That night I learned yet once again what I had been struggling to realize for many years: that prayer is not merely the saying of words; it is the experiencing of God. Both forms of prayer were real, but the latter moved upon a higher plane. It was prayer lifted to the level of worship.

Worship is the response of created man to his Creator. It is man ceasing to be an alien in the universe and becoming instead at home with God. It is man in his finitude becoming aware of his kinship with infinite Reality. Prayer does not always move in this realm of worship, but it always should. Sometimes it is only a rudimentary expression of real kinship with the Eternal, as in a prayer that is merely a habit, a duty, or a form. Now, however, we have had an awakening to the possibility of meeting God face to face and have come to realize that this can be the overtone of all our praying. Our everyday prayers can be transformed as we realize in them the four dynamic spiritual movements of our souls toward God which were presented at the close of the last chapter. Let us now consider them more fully and seek to understand how, even at the beginning of the life of devotion, our vocal prayers can be permanently lifted to a higher level as they are motivated by these dynamics of the spirit.

1. STILLNESS—FROM SURFACE SELF TO GOD-INTENDED SELF

a. The Veil of the Temple. When the high priest once a year entered the Holy of Holies in Jerusalem, he dropped the veil of the temple in place behind him that the world might be shut out, and that he might be shut in alone with the Shekinah of God. Even so, all true seekers of the holy Presence must grow still, turn inward, and drop the veil of the temple of prayer behind them if they would truly pray.

Breaking the vivid stream of consciousness with which we enter our sanctuary is a primary problem for the man who prays. When we come into the place of prayer, we of course bring ourselves in with us, and our minds are filled with the stream of consciousness which has claimed our attention. Perhaps we have just driven our automobile home through the rush-hour traffic. Speeding cars, flashing traffic signals, and impatient policemen have been vividly perceived. Our feelings may have been stirred by irritating delays. Perhaps there was a radio in the car, and, as we turned it on, disturbing news arrested us. In the background of our homeward drive were all the tensions from the activities of our busy day. Now we find ourselves alone in our room. If we were to begin to pray immediately, all the wheels would still be going around in our mind. Fragments of memory would flash across the screen of our attention. No matter how we tried to say words of prayer, this vivid background would be too much for us, and the prayer would probably be merely a routine form of words.

We must deliberately shift mental gears. We must break across the vivid stream of our consciousness. Our first act must be to drop a veil between ourselves and the world. At once it must be said that this does not mean that we are to retreat into an ivory tower permanently detached from the world. It should not mean that we regard prayer as a watertight compartment unrelated to the flow of life. It does mean, however, that we temporarily cut ourselves off from the world in order to return, empowered, to its demands. The interplay of life and prayer is fundamental; but in order that prayer may play upon life, it is necessary for us to go apart from the clamor and pressure of our daily existence, and pass from our surface self to our deeper self. We must share the high wisdom which led Jesus so often to go apart to mountainside, desert, or garden to pray.

There are two ways we can alter the current of our consciousness: the first is by slowing down the pace of our thoughts and laying aside the hurry of the day as we would remove an outer garment; and the second, when the mind has thus been prepared for the rhythm of greater thoughts, is by dropping the veil of some new experience to shut out the mental pictures with which we entered the sanctuary. Horace Bushnell described conversion as "the expulsive power of a new affection." Often when we cannot drive thoughts from our mind, we can replace them with some more vital experience.

Some form of soul preparation is valuable for us all before we pray. We sit quietly in our sanctuary of solitude, relaxed in the conscious peace of the sacred time that we have set apart for the Eternal. Slowly and deliberately we fill our minds with some intimation of the Divine. About us are our favorite aids to devotion. We reach out a hand to open a hymnbook and turn its pages seeking some verse that perfectly catches up our need and lifts it into the place of the available resources from on high. The keynote for an entire devotional period of prayer is often sounded through the words and remembered music of a well-loved hymn. Or, on some other occasion, we open a book of prayers that has become like the voice of a friend overheard in the sacred intimacy of his soul talk with his God. We feel that we stand upon holy ground, and read with deepening reverence, thinking our way into his prayer, making his words our own. Sometimes our glance lingers longer on a picture. Perchance it is Holman Hunt's "Light of the World." It is so familiar; we have known it since childhood; but this day it speaks with new poignancy—the hand lifted and knocking, the rich meaning of every object, the closed door, the lighted lantern, the coming dawn. But what draws us most compellingly is the eyes of the Man of Galilee. His hand is knocking, and His eyes are seeking. What are they seeking in my heart? What do they expect to see in me? Unwittingly we find our memories stirring and our lips quietly repeating His words: "Behold, I stand at the door, and knock: if any man hear my voice, and open the door, I will come in to him." (Rev. 3:20.)

Sometimes it is not one of these aids to devotion upon our prayer table to which we turn before our prayer, but a window, where God's universe opens before us.

Once there were two friends facing a tense and difficult hour. Finally one said, "What do you see?"

"I see the lighted candles and their reflections in the windows," the other answered.

"Blow out the candles," said his friend. "Come near the window." For a moment they stood silently, side by side, until their eyes became accustomed to the soft light of the sky. Then he continued, "Now what do you see?"

"I see the stars."

Sometimes it is good for us to turn out our man-made lights and stand looking at the eternal silence and the abiding steadfastness of God's stars. While we must beware of distractions from the external world, it is valuable for many of us to stand at our window for a moment in preparation for prayer. For one who has eyes to see, it is but a step from nature to nature's God.

But for all of us the Bible brings most frequently that preparation of the mind and heart which is the prelude to real prayer. We may read it in some planned sequence, or we may turn to those parts which contain the richest profusion of living insights and compelling truths; but we must read it devotionally, that it may become a living Word of God speaking some stimulating message to us as we seek His Presence.

b. The Art of Stillness. After we have in some way shifted our mental gears and dropped a veil between ourselves and the world, we come to prayer itself. Whether our prayer be during an extended period of devotion or in the briefest moment of worship, it should always begin with stillness. Fénelon once said: "How rare it is to find a soul quiet enough to hear God speak!" The psalmist gave to us God's gentle command: "Be still, and know that I am God." (Ps. 46:10.) Whittier beautifully expresses the spirit of all true prayer:

> Drop Thy still dews of quietness,
>   Till all our strivings cease;
> Take from our souls the strain and stress,
> And let our ordered lives confess
>   The beauty of Thy peace.

If we are to approach God and possess a deeper and more real sense of His Presence, we must give ourselves utterly to Him in quiet reflection. In the heart of Crawford Notch up in the White Mountains there is a little pool formed by the waters of the Saco River. The mountain winds are usually rushing down through the Notch and ruffling the waters with a continuous disturbance. But at times the winds are hushed and the waters still, and then its quiet mirror catches and reflects perfectly the towering cliffs of Mount Webster and the infinite blue deeps of the sky above. Only when the winds of the world that blow across our lives are quieted can we grow still enough to reflect the Infinite in the deeps of our lives.

This discipline of quietness is a necessary prelude to the appreciation of any value in life. We go to a symphony concert. Only rarely do the first passages of the symphony sweep irresistibly into our hearts. Too many of us bring in with us the rush and hurry of our getting to the hall. We have not yet escaped from the domination of those pressing concerns which still race through our minds. But by degrees we grow still; our heated hearts grow calm; and the insistent beauty of the music displaces the torrent of our inner turmoil. We become aware of a center of beauty about which to pull ourselves together. As the stillness deepens, our hearts open more perfectly to the thrill of the music itself. There comes, at length, an exquisite moment when in the depth of stillness the music enthralls us and speaks to our very hearts in the perfect moment of the concert. Only in such stillness does classic music reveal its full beauty.

Even so is prayer. We grow quiet that we may mirror the profound and infinite heights of God; we grow still that we may become more nearly attuned to His inner symphony. Life is so strenuous for most people today that there is dire need for inner quietness. All of us are driven by many tasks and constantly assailed by a stream of noisy stimuli. If ever a people needed to "study to be quiet," we are they. It is out of our rush and tumult that so many of us kneel for a hurried moment of prayer. We cannot deeply see God under these circumstances, any more than a hurried tourist can really apprehend Reims Cathedral.

The first essential, then, as we kneel to pray is to grow quiet. We do not hurry to speak. We let our body relax. We consciously loosen the tension of every muscle. We quiet our mind in the realization that for a few moments there is just one thing to claim our attention—prayer. All the responsibilities of the day are laid aside; we are at the supreme business of our life. We are alone, at worship, with our God. Our mind has been like a mainspring wound tight too long and ready to snap; now we release its tension and let it run down. We do not struggle with our thoughts, or strive to dismiss them from our mind. We just let go of them. For these few sacred moments we are still and know that God is.

c. Introversion. This process of stilling the soul and turning inward to the deeps is called "introversion." It is not to be confused with introspection, which is the different process of analyzing and looking at ourselves. It is an Upper Room of the Presence of God and not a Hall of Mirrors in which we see only ourselves. In stillness we withdraw from external things and concern with the surface self to some awareness of eternal Reality and a centering down in our deeper selves.

As we grow still, we tend to leave the surface self with its quick reactions to every external stimulus. We enter the inner kingdom of real personality, for, after all, life has two levels of reality: one aspect is the surface self interacting with an outer world; the other, the essential self aware of conscious experiences and eternal values. We live in both worlds, but our true home is in the deeps within. Here are found thoughts, judgments, character, love, hope, memory, creative imagination, purposes, clear insights, ideals, organizing sentiments, and that sense of continuity and self-identity that makes all these experiences the possession of an enduring self. This is the real world. In prayer we enter it and shut the door upon the clamorous impacts of the world of sense perception.

When we consciously enter the inner realm of selfhood, we become aware of our place in a universe of personality. The fact of which we are most indubitably sure is our own self-consciousness. This is a primary reality at the very center of our experience. It is a fact created by the mysterious power of the World Ground. Intuitively we know that we are not cosmic accidents. We are one expression of the intention of the Creative Process that has produced us. From the Creator personality has sprung; in the Creator personality must eternally exist. Upon this primary insight there arises an inescapable sense of possible contact between the praying self and the Personal Creator through whose will we exist. To grow still in prayer is to become aware of the deep self and its possible communion with the cosmic Personality, God. Jesus suggested this reality when He began the classic prayer of Christianity with the words "Our Father." The filial sense of our sonship and of God's Fatherhood is basic to true prayer. Bosanquet has pointed out that salvation is the process of becoming at home in the universe. Prayer is the process of becoming at home with God.

2. RECOLLECTION—FROM SELF-CENTEREDNESS TO GOD-CENTEREDNESS

Jan Smuts has said, "The disease of our age is fragmentation." We are all aware that some profound dissociation is tearing apart the lives of multitudes of people in our civilization. Karen Horney, one of the most penetrating psychiatrists of our day, points out that the basic neurotic conflict of our times arises from the feeling that man is alienated from himself, from others, and from the universe; that he is helpless and insecure; that he is fearful and beset by anxiety. Man is at war within himself and involved in deep conflict. Only the reassurances of religion can enable a man to pull himself together about a center in which he can place absolute confidence.

Again, our culture is disintegrating into a terrible nihilism. We are living in an uprooted age which has lost contact with its foundations. Paul Tillich points out that the profound disturbance in the heart of our world is due to the illusion that modern civilization is so powerful that it can conquer finiteness, sin, and tragedy, and thus enable us to achieve security. But blow upon blow is undermining our confidence in this illusion. Many are being driven into despair and cynicism. Religion, and only religion, has the power to answer the profound demands of life in a time like this.

What is needed is a return to the eternal foundations. There was an eternity before the worlds were formed. There is an eternity which will last even when our world is destroyed. Even if the present age crumbles into chaos and dissolves into tragedy, we have an everlasting foundation in the Presence of the Eternal God. He it is who has created man, and He it is upon whom we depend for ultimate uplifting. "Underneath are the Everlasting Arms," and round about us always is the strength of God. This is the order to which we as human beings belong. Through God's grace we participate in that which is infinite. Even if the present world is destroyed, there is a realm neither transitory nor self-destructive nor tragic.

It is a return to the tremendous assurances of our Christian faith that steadies us at the heart of the experience of prayer as worship. This collecting of life about the central core that assures the integrity and preservation of our personality is called "recollection." This word is not used in the sense of remembrance. It is used rather in its primary sense to mean re-collecting ourselves about the ultimate center of our being which is God. There are many degrees of recollection, but it is an objective that should be clearly in our mind at every stage of prayer from the least developed and most spontaneous to the very highest level. God-centered praying is worship at its truest and best.

The discipline of recollection is a necessary prelude to the direct contemplative awareness of the Divine Presence. Like every true emphasis in prayer, it is more than a part of the worship experience. It is one of the central demands of Christianity itself. We must never forget that the life process parallels the prayer process and accompanies it at every point. Our objective is to collect our entire lives about God as the living center of our being. It is this goal held steadily before us that lifts conversational prayer, ritual prayer, corporate worship, or the sacraments up to the level of vital worship. No elaborate changes or techniques are needed, but rather do we need clarity of insight into the vital process at the very heart of all true religion—this turning of our being toward the Eternal. We shall let the word "recollection" stand for this emphasis in our experience and then strive for it in all of our life of prayer.

Here is a preacher going into his pulpit on a Sunday morning. He has been busy with many concerns in his church. He has paused to meet with an important committee. He has been so rushed that he is worried about whether his sermon is adequately prepared and is tense with anxiety as he faces his holy responsibility. He moves into his pulpit, but his ministry is not God-centered; he is not in a state of recollection. This is not to say that he should be in some abnormal state. Rather is recollection the form of that healthy normality of which he is desperately in need. His present disintegrated, distracted, and dissociated state is the abnormal one.

Here is another minister whose process of worship, stillness, introversion, and recollection began the night before. He has maintained a depth of silence and a continuity of prayer. His sermon is brooded upon meditatively and prayerfully. In the morning he has walked alone with God. In his study, before entering the pulpit, he has prayed until his whole being is transformed by the awareness of the Divine Presence. He has forgotten himself. He is recollected about the deep center of his being. He is quiet in soul, in communion with his God.

Even so every Christian ought continually to seek this condition of inner poise, steadying certitude, and living awareness of God, which will enable him to move among the busy throngs with "the dust of the world on his garments" and yet carry his sacred shrine with him everywhere. What help parents, teachers, businessmen—in fact, all of us—can find in thus achieving a state of deep recollection in prayer! Recollection is a sacred obligation resting upon all who would grow in their Christian life. It is one of the major objectives of all prayer, to be held constantly before us no matter in what form of prayer we may be engaged.

3. AWARENESS—FROM SELF-CONSCIOUSNESS TO GOD-CONSCIOUSNESS

Closely allied to recollection is the end product of this process, which is some degree of awareness of God. Recollection is the process of turning Godward, of concentrating our attention by a willed effort, or through love and adoration, upon God in any of the aspects of His Divine Being. Awareness is the resulting experience in which we rest in some radiant consciousness of His Presence. It is always the gift of God's grace that illumines us as we pray. In its developed form this is the climax of contemplation. But to some extent it should be present, at least in its incipiency, in every form of prayer, if prayer is to be lifted to the level of real worship and not to be merely the saying of words. The very holding of the deep convictions of our faith strongly centered in our thoughts when we pray is an elementary form of awareness. The never-varying conviction that whenever we pray, whether we have any emotional feeling or not, we are nevertheless praying in the faith that God is there is the very basis of making prayer real. The growing insights that emerge as we meditate are on the verge of this experience. The source of all worship is some awareness of God as present. It is some touch of God upon the soul that summons us to every real experience of prayer. All prayer is rooted in the faith, held in the very ground of the soul, that it corresponds with the Eternal. This is the core of individual worship. With the fullness of this experience we shall be concerned in our discussion of contemplation.

4. RESPONSE—FROM SELF-WILL TO GOD'S WILL

After we have in any degree become humbly aware of a direct and most sacred relationship of our souls to God, we are called to make some act of response. No prayer is true prayer until it issues in an act of response. It is never to be enjoyed for itself alone. The inescapable reaction of any degree of communion with the Eternal is the call for life-adjustment to His will.

Our response may be merely the appropriation of the joy and peace which come from the recognition of the nearness of God's Presence to our lives. Or it may be a profound humility awakened by the contrast of what a man feels about himself as over against God. This is the motivation of the process of purgation, whereby we strive to purge our lives of all that hinders our communion with God. This demand will deepen into a call for the total dedication of the finite will to the Infinite will. This is an essential interior act of all Christianity. At its highest this process of self-giving will lead to the place where the egocentric self, and its interests and plans, must be lost in a more perfect adjustment of life to God's will.

Again, our response may be the awakening in us of those flames of living love whereby we make answer to the greatness of the love which we have found in the heart of God. Or still again, the response may be the consciousness of contact with the flow of God's power in answer to some petition which we lift to Him in prayer. Or it may be that we shall respond with intercession, through which we express our loving co-operation with God's creative intention. At its highest our response may make us channels of the redeeming outreach of God to mankind as we share his vicarious love.

But whatever the form of our response, we are called to appropriate to our own lives the truth which we have glimpsed in prayer. This is one of the essential objectives to be held constantly in mind. Prayer is a creative process with practical consequences in the life of every man who truly prays.

CHAPTER IX

Practicing the Life of Devotion

VOCAL PRAYER—TECHNIQUES

And he spake a parable unto them to this end, that men ought always to pray, and not to faint. —Luke 18:1

THE MOVEMENT OF THE SOUL TOWARD GOD IN STILLNESS, RECOL-lection, awareness, and response can begin even as we make use of the very simplest forms of prayer. The important thing is to lift them from the dead level of the mere saying of words, or "saying our prayers," up to some degree of prayer as worship.

One time I stood in the corridor of a hospital, outside the door of a room into which I must go as pastor. Within was a cherished friend who was suffering from an incurable disease. The doctor had just told me that his end was not far off, and I stood there conscious of my impotence. What had I as a human being to offer him in circumstances like these? In such a moment our hearts instinctively turn Godward in prayer. For years in such crises of need I had offered a sentence prayer which was a direct supplication for God to help, and I still know that this type of prayer offered in terrible sincerity is valuable and valid. But this time my prayer moved on an even more effective plane as a worship experience.

For a moment I paused and grew still. Though the nurses were hurrying down the corridor past me on their errands of mercy, for a brief moment I relaxed the tension of every responsibility and just grew quiet. Then I offered a brief act of recollection, by which I strove to center my thoughts on

God. I found myself repeating the verse: "Fear thou not; for I am with thee: be not dismayed; for I am thy God: I will strengthen thee; yea, I will help thee; yea, I will uphold thee with the right hand of my righteousness." (Isa. 41:10.)

There came, even in this brief moment, a consciousness that I was not alone. I responded to this, appropriating it to my need. God was with me as I stood outside the door. He was within by the side of the patient suffering there. Neither he nor I need be afraid or overwhelmed. God would see us through, and there would never come a moment so terrific in its exaction but that, from the mysterious inner resources of the human spirit, God would release adequate strength with which to go through it. The Divine Companion was by my friend's side as if saying, "I will help you." That meant there were two there to bear the burden. Christ was under it with him, and by His mighty power and through His love He would help so mightily that the burden could be borne. And when the end came, still would He be uplifting him. Underneath would be the Everlasting Arms. He would be lifting him up tenderly, setting his feet upon the upward way that leads to the new radiance of immortal life.

All this flashed through my mind in an instant of time. Then I said Amen and went inside—and we were not alone.

1. ACTS OF DEVOTION

Such an experience lifts ordinary vocal prayer up to the level of true worship. We may call it an "act of devotion." It is a form of prayer so simple and yet so real that every Christian should train himself to use it frequently. These are its parts:

a. *Stillness.* Let us grow quiet and relaxed even if we have only a few seconds in which to pray. The stillness may be the most real part of this form of prayer.

b. *Recollection,* through a brief prayer, which must be objective and God-centered. Sentence prayers are so often subjective, centering in ourselves and our needs. What is needed

115

here is the turning of our souls from ourselves, as the subject of our prayer, to God, as the object of our worship. Momentarily we lift our minds Godward by repeating a meaningful verse of scripture—for example: "Come unto me, all ye that labour and are heavy laden, and I will give you rest." (Matt. 11:28.) We make these words the means of our communion with God. They unite our hearts to Him. We become, even in this brief space of time, more God-centered. This therefore becomes for us a more profound form of prayer than self-centered words of supplication. We can use any appropriate Bible verse, or a stanza of a hymn, or some brief ritual prayer. If none of these come to mind, we can use a worshipful sentence prayer of our own. To prepare ourselves for our acts of devotion we may write out verses on cards to be carried in pocket or purse. Better still, we may memorize them and have them always available for the enrichment of our life of prayer.

c. *Awareness,* through a momentary realization that we are praying in the very presence of the eternal God. Our only action here is trustful waiting and the turning of our heart toward Him in loving attention. Frequently this awareness will not even be explicit, but as we look back on the experience we shall know that God was with us as we prayed. Through His grace a new tone has been communicated to our consciousness: we are less burdened, more at peace, more steady, more confident. God has, in fact, secretly illumined our hearts.

d. *Response.* We make an application to our present life situation. This can be done very simply and immediately. The whole genius of an act of devotion is its brevity and directness. Momentarily we have become God-centered through prayer and through realization of God's nearness. Now we apply this insight to whatever problem or condition we are facing. We say, "If this scripture promise, which I have used as a brief prayer of communion to unite my heart to God, is true, and if its reality can be made available for me now through the nearness of His Presence, then God can take hold of and change my life situation." Thus we meditate briefly about the application of our verse to our personal experience. We talk with God in quiet, confident communion. Then we say Amen and go back to meet life with quiet inner steadiness and new spiritual strength.

Whenever we raise our hearts toward God, even in the simplest expression through ejaculations, words of recall, brief aspirations, or spontaneous supplications, it will help us if we can consciously train ourselves to express as many of these four Godward movements of the soul as possible in our prayer. Usually, however, we make one of the four central in any one act of devotion, and group the other three around it. Thus acts of devotion become the means of expressing varied moods of the soul as it reaches toward communion with the Divine. A few selections that can be used as the brief central prayer are listed below. Others should be collected in our prayer notebooks that our minds and hearts may be prepared for a richer life of worshipful prayer.

ACTS OF STILLNESS

Be still, and know that I am God. (Ps. 46:10.)

It is good that man should both hope and quietly wait for the salvation of the Lord. (Lam. 3:26.)

Of quiet and confidence: In quietness and in confidence shall be your strength. (Isa. 30:15.)

Of peace: Thou wilt keep him in perfect peace, whose mind is stayed on thee: because he trusteth in thee. (Isa. 26:3.)

Peace I leave with you, my peace I give unto you: not as the world giveth, give I unto you. Let not your heart be troubled, neither let it be afraid. (John 14:27.)

ACTS OF RECOLLECTION

He that dwelleth in the secret place of the most High shall abide under the shadow of the Almighty. (Ps. 91:1.)

Of faith: The eternal God is thy refuge, and underneath are the everlasting arms. (Deut. 33:27.)

Of affirmation: Thou art worthy, O Lord, to receive glory and honour and power: for thou hast created all things, and for thy pleasure they are and were created. (Rev. 4:11.)

Alleluia: for the Lord God omnipotent reigneth. (Rev. 19:6.)

Of praise and thanksgiving: Bless the Lord, O my soul: and all that is within me, bless his holy name. (Ps. 103:1.)

Of adoration: Christ, we do all adore Thee!

ACTS OF AWARENESS

Fear thou not; for I am with thee: be not dismayed; for I am thy God: I will strengthen thee; yea, I will help thee; yea, I will uphold thee with the right hand of my righteousness. (Isa. 41:10.)

Lo, I am with you always, even unto the end of the world. (Matt. 28:20.)

Am I a God at hand, saith the Lord, and not a God afar off? Can any hide himself in secret places that I shall not see him? saith the Lord. Do not I fill heaven and earth? saith the Lord. (Jer. 23:23-24.)

The Spirit of God dwelleth in you. (I Cor. 3:16.)

Of invocation: Hear my prayer, O Lord . . . : in thy faithfulness answer me. (Ps. 143:1.)

Out of the depths have I cried unto thee, O Lord. Lord, hear my voice: let thine ears be attentive to the voice of my supplications. (Ps. 130:1-2.)

The hymns "Come, Holy Ghost, in Love" and "Spirit of God, Descend upon My Heart."

Of love: Who shall separate us from the love of Christ? . . . For I am persuaded, that neither death, nor life . . . shall be able to separate us from the love of God, which is in Christ Jesus our Lord. (Rom. 8:35, 38, 39.)

Of illumination: For God, who commanded the light to shine out of darkness, hath shined in our hearts, to give the light of the knowledge of the glory of God in the face of Jesus Christ. (II Cor. 4:6.)

ACTS OF RESPONSE

I delight to do thy will, O my God. (Ps. 40:8.)

God is love; and he that dwelleth in love dwelleth in God, and God in him. (I John 4:16.)

Of confession: Against thee, thee only, have I sinned, and done this evil in thy sight. (Ps. 51:4.)

Of forgiveness: Father, forgive them; for they know not what they do. (Luke 23:34.)

Of cleansing: Collect for Purity of Heart.

Of consecration: I beseech you therefore, brethren, by the mercies of God, that ye present your bodies a living sacrifice, holy, acceptable unto God, which is your reasonable service. (Rom. 12:1.)

Of vicariousness: I am crucified with Christ: nevertheless I live; yet not I, but Christ liveth in me. (Gal. 2:20.)

Acts of devotion should become a living part of our everyday life. The moment in the day when life is most disturbed and prayer seems most incongruous is the very time to stand still, steady ourselves, and use an act of devotion to recall ourselves to the consciousness of God. Once I suggested this to a prayer seminar in my church, and the very next day a woman of the group had this experience. She had arisen early, done her regular work, and hung her washing out on the line. It was a day in March when the sky was blue, the sun shining, and the wind blowing. She looked out the window at the white clothes and was pleased with her accomplishment. A few moments later when she glanced again she saw that the clothesline had broken. The March wind had been too much for it; the white wash was in the mud. For a moment she almost lost control of herself in irritation and resentment. Then she recalled the suggestion about prayer and, yielding to a sudden impulse, stood still in the middle of the kitchen floor, grew quiet, and repeated as her brief prayer the words: "Be still, and know that I am God." For a few seconds she realized its meaning for her life then and there. The flood of her quick emotion slowly ebbed away. Her inner poise returned. Her spiritual perspective restored control to the situation. Then she said Amen. As she told me of the experience later, she said that she laughed out loud at the contrast of this domestic episode and her standing in the middle of her room praying. And yet she said that it had brought to her as never before the consciousness of how prayer and life should be interwoven constantly.

Acts of devotion are as simple and homespun as that. On the other hand, they can express our profoundest outreach to God in prayer and become the vehicle of our loving attention to Him as we approach the very summit of contemplation.

2. PLACING OURSELVES CONSCIOUSLY IN GOD'S PRESENCE

Whenever we come to one of our regular devotional periods, whether we are going to pray in the free conversation of the colloquy or through meditation, the whole experience can be lifted to a higher plane if we will deliberately take time to place ourselves consciously in the Presence of God before we pray. He is with us always, but we, on our part, must take time to become aware of this mighty fact. For this purpose may I suggest a pattern which has proved to be unusually helpful: the offering of four separate acts of devotion in a planned and unhurried progression as a prelude to the prayer.

a. An Act of Stillness, through which we turn our hearts toward God in quiet confidence. This may be offered as we approach the place where we are to pray. We may pause a moment, stand still, grow relaxed in body and quiet in spirit. We then offer as a brief prayer one of the scripture verses suggested above under "Acts of Stillness." We are aware of the peace of God that passes understanding as it enters and stills our hearts. We respond to this movement of the spirit by dedicating the next few moments to the quiet leisure of unhurried prayer. At times, instead of thus pausing and offering an explicit act of stillness, we may express the spirit of this movement of our souls toward God through the stillness experienced in the three other acts of devotion.

b. An Act of Recollection, through which we turn our hearts to God in reverence. Following stillness we offer a brief, objective prayer expressed in one of the selections listed above under "Acts of Recollection." Or we may repeat the Sanctus:

"Therefore with angels and archangels, and with all the company of heaven, we laud and magnify Thy glorious Name, evermore praising Thee, and saying: Holy, holy, holy, Lord God of Hosts, heaven and earth are full of Thy glory. Glory be to Thee, O Lord most high! Amen." Or we may use such a scripture verse as: "Lord, thou hast been our dwelling place in all generations. Before the mountains were brought forth, or ever thou hadst formed the earth and the world, even from everlasting to everlasting, thou art God." (Ps. 90:1-2.) As we thus center our minds on God, we make explicit our awareness that He is with us always and that prayer means an approach to the place of His very nearness. We find ourselves responding to the drawing of His Spirit, and we yield ourselves more perfectly to His leading.

c. An Act of Confession, through which we turn our hearts toward God in sincerity. Penitence, contrition, aspiration, confidence of forgiveness, or resolution may be the mood of this prayer. Following our second act of devotion we again grow deeply quiet, and then as our brief prayer we repeat the Collect for Purity of Heart, a general confession, or perchance some scripture verses like these: "Create in me a clean heart, O God; and renew a right spirit within me. Cast me not away from thy presence; and take not thy holy spirit from me." (Ps. 51:10-11.) We are aware of the gracious act of God in cleansing our hearts. Then we respond with deep appreciation for the mighty grace of His love, which condescends to meet and forgive His weak and finite children so often, and to grant us the unthinkable privilege of entering into communion with Him in prayer.

d. An Act of Invocation, through which we move toward God in humility. This is a spontaneous supplication for God to draw near and help us as we pray. For the fourth time we still our hearts, and then perhaps repeat: "Behold, I stand at the door, and knock: if any man hear my voice, and open the door, I will come in to him." (Rev. 3:20*a.*) And then we add in the words of the hymns:

> O come to my heart, Lord Jesus,
> There is room in my heart for Thee.[1]

Or we may repeat:

> Come, Holy Spirit, heavenly Dove,
> With all Thy quickening powers;
> Kindle a flame of sacred love
> In these cold hearts of ours.[2]

Or again we may use our own words to ask the grace of His deeper coming into our hearts to help us as we pray. Our awareness of how near God is has deepened constantly as we have offered these acts of devotion. Our response to His nearness now opens our hearts in expectant receptivity as we enter upon our conversational prayer or our meditation.

This succession of four acts of devotion might on occasion become the fullness of a prayer experience, for there can be joined to each act a brief meditation, or colloquy, in which the richness of its meaning may be unfolded. Surely their use day by day would habituate the soul to a deeper life of prayer and lead us toward the higher forms of devotion to which we are seeking to advance.

3. WORSHIP THROUGH RITUAL PRAYER

Real stimulus for the life of prayer can be found for every person in the use of the historic material of ritual which his part of the Christian Church has preserved. The use of Morning and Evening Prayer from the *Book of Common Prayer* for personal devotions throughout an entire year would be an unusually rewarding worship experience. It would lead us to read the succession of great scripture passages through which is unfolded the majestic panorama of the supreme revelations of God. At the same time it would familiarize the mind

[1] Emily E. S. Elliott.
[2] Isaac Watts.

with many classic prayers that have helped Christians through the ages.

In addition to the use of ritual material we could well deepen our worship by learning the structure of the type of ritual prayer known as a "collect" and then in devout meditation spending time in expressing our reach Godward through this form. Or again, we might on occasion give our devotional experience another ritual form—a litany. We might choose some meaningful refrain and then reverently express our thoughts and feelings in a succession of brief prayers, concluding each with a chosen refrain. How well this is adapted to a prayer of thanksgiving or, for that matter, a prayer of self-examination!

The use of any ritual form merely as a vocal prayer, the words of which are repeated without much attention to their meaning, has a certain value; but how much greater is its value when it is used worshipfully! If we let the soul grow quiet and the repetition be unhurried, if we direct the mind to the meaning of the noble phrases that are repeated and pause between each of them to let their meaning sink into our soul, if we let our whole soul be turned Godward as we pray— then our vocal prayer is lifted to true fulfillment in a worshipful experience.

4. THE COLLOQUY

Basic to prayer at all levels is the pouring out of our souls in intimate, spontaneous, heart-to-heart prayer. This is the colloquy, or conversational prayer. Here we express any and all moods and aspirations of the soul at worship, together with our petitions, intercessions, confessions, and resolutions.

This prayer, too, can be transformed from a primitive level of vocal prayer to one that includes and expresses stillness, recollection, awareness, and response. Here again we may prepare our hearts for our free conversation with God by first placing ourselves consciously in His Presence through the use of the suggested sequence of four acts of devotion.

Through this preparation of our souls our colloquy will be immeasurably deepened and enriched. If we further train ourselves to worship ever more profoundly as we thus pray, the element of mere words will gradually be transformed into the simple waiting of our souls on God that can lead us into His very Presence.

Petition and intercession form real parts of our conversational prayers. Petition begins as an attempt to fortify and enhance our own personalities. It can rise from the stage of a primitive request to the level of a supplication for God to grant unto us the rich gifts of the Spirit. So also can intercession be transformed from the level of primitive sympathy for a group to a sharing of the redemptive love of God.

The form that we use is not as important as the reality of the Godward movement of our hearts. We are on a pilgrimage from self to God, and every time we pray we discipline ourselves for higher experiences on the upward trail. All Christians who have made prayer real through the ages have learned in some way to place themselves consciously in the Presence of God as they prayed, and thus they have lifted their prayer to the level of living worship.

CHAPTER X

Creative Meditation

MENTAL PRAYER—ITS MOTIVATION

Let the words of my mouth, and the meditation of my heart, be acceptable in thy sight, O Lord, my strength, and my redeemer.
—Ps. 19:14

IN DEEPEST REALITY, PRAYER IS TALKING WITH GOD AS WITH A familiar friend. If He is real to us and our souls wait quietly before Him, we talk with Him as naturally and spontaneously as with the dearest human personality whose friendship we treasure. This is the secret known to multitudes of Christians in all ages. It is an experience which we all need to recapture. We can do this through mastering the art of meditation.

1. OUR OBJECTIVES IN MEDITATION

Meditation is the great training ground for our souls as we strive to reach the goal of a more God-centered form of prayer through recollection. Our first aim is to develop a new form of spiritual attention whereby we learn to control our minds and direct them to look steadily at God. This process will be hard at first because our mental muscles are flabby. If we are to concentrate our attention on some spiritual object, we must learn to control and direct our thoughts, our imagination, our memories, our feelings, and our wills. We must strive to achieve a psychological focus of all our mental powers.

Our second objective is to achieve a new and more direct form of perception. We want to discover truths for ourselves firsthand. This, too, will be difficult for us, for we are accustomed, in this age of mass information, to get so much of our knowledge and so many of our ideas from others. Then, too, we are conditioned by the scientific spirit which thinks that it understands reality when it has learned the current label which superficial thought pastes over the facts. The vision of God comes only to those whose minds have been prepared and enriched by brooding long on spiritual things.

Our final purpose is to quicken our response to God and to His will for our lives. Meditation in prayer differs from ordinary meditation in that it aims to be life-changing and creative, and not merely speculative. We use it to purify our senses, to educate our wills, and to bring about a growing adjustment of ourselves to the Reality which we perceive. True meditation is always dynamic in character. In it we discipline our minds to the mind of God and our lives to His will.

Concerning it W. E. Orchard says:

Meditation is rightly called mental prayer, for it is a type of prayer in which we use our minds with a determinate and ordered purpose; and it is therefore a type of mental activity, especially for our generation, so dependent upon printed or outside prescription, rarely employed and almost atrophied. . . . The intellectual activity which might be employed on meditation could exhaust any powers that a trained philosopher or informed theologian possessed. What might be contributed by the imaginative faculties could employ the highest powers possessed by an artistic, poetic, or dramatic genius. The volitional energy which might be manufactured in meditation might, in the hands of a resolute personality, not only change character but mould history. Unfortunately, however, most of us are more deficient than gifted in one, two, or all three of these elements. If we set ourselves to think, we find we can think of nothing; if we set ourselves to think about some religious subject, we find our minds tempted to think of almost anything else. Again, we find that while we can feel strongly enough about some wrong done to us, to feel rightly and deeply, to order, about something that ought to move us leaves us only hard, cold, and dry. And when it comes to making resolutions, if we can think, at the moment, of any worth making, we often not only forget to carry them out, we even forget beyond recall what was the resolution we made.[1]

2. THE PRACTICE OF MEDITATION

There are many specific methods of Christian meditation. As we now share them, may we find many fruitful suggestions to enrich whatever method of prayer we build for ourselves. We should not try to use every suggestion in any one experience. This would be as undesirable as it would be impossible. But we should have available a wealth of rich alternatives awaiting our free choice whenever we pray. Let us experiment with them, use first one then another. Let us keep our prayer lives vital and varied. We must not mind if some of the methods seem a little unnatural at first. All of these have proved their value to multitudes of earnest Christians, and there is help in them for us if we will only persevere until they become native in our experience.

We may, if we wish, consider meditation a preparation for prayer. At first, while we are becoming accustomed to it, we may write out our meditations, or we may depend entirely on meditated readings. We may prefer to start by using some of the meditative processes, which are to be presented, in only a partial way. In the hope, however, that we shall come to the place where meditation becomes a fruitful way of prayer for us, let us now examine several methods of mental prayer.

3. MEDITATED READINGS

One way to begin this method of prayer is to start with a very simple process of Bible reading. We choose some passage and read it over slowly and thoughtfully. Then we grow still in a moment of prayer and talk with God about its spiritual meanings. Finally we end the experience with a spontaneous conversational prayer which includes some definite promise to carry its implications out into action in our lives.

Another way is through the meditated reading of material in a prayer book, a devotional manual, or a Bible commentary

---

[1] *Prayer* (New York: Harper & Bros., 1930), pp. 107-8. Used by permission.

in which the background, meaning, and teaching of a passage of Scripture are worked out in detail. Certain parts of the next chapter of this book might also be used as the basis of such meditation. After a prayer for God to help and guide us, or after the use of specific acts of devotion, we read the passage in the book. Then we sit quietly in a period of reflection or brooding about the subject and its meaning for our lives. We end this period by choosing some small action which will apply what we have learned. We promise God that we will, by His help, carry out this new resolution. Then we end our meditation with spontaneous prayer.

A further variation of this practice is to divide our consideration of the subject into two parts. (1) We write down what we have learned from the passage which we have read meditatively, together with our own comments on it. Then (2) we reflect upon this subject which has now been opened up to our inward gaze. We draw out the corollaries of the truths considered, especially questioning how they relate to our lives or what we can do about them. Then we proceed to our resolutions and closing prayer. This approach will give excellent training for our progress to the place where meditation can become a normal part of our devotional lives.

The meditated use of ritual material can be exceedingly rewarding. For example, instead of repeating the Lord's Prayer suppose that we were to say it slowly, taking time to meditate upon each word or significant phrase. If we were to take ten or fifteen minutes in which to say the Lord's Prayer thus thoughtfully, it would forever afterward have for us a far richer personal significance. On some occasions, as its deeper meanings unfold for us, we might find that one word or phrase would occupy us for an entire devotional period. We could then continue with the next word, or phrase, at a succeeding time of prayer. There is another way of saying the Lord's Prayer which has been practiced by Christians for centuries: to say one word of the Lord's Prayer between one breath (in and out) and another, thinking about it just for this brief period, and then continuing with the next word. This slowing down of the tempo of our devotions cannot but make our vocal prayers more real, and what has been said concerning the Lord's Prayer can be applied to other meaningful prayers that we repeat.

4. THE TRIANGLE OF MEDITATION

We have already seen the analogy of prayer to a triangle in considering intercession. In his book *Living Religion* Hornell Hart some years ago presented this suggestion:

True meditation involves a triangular relationship. At the apex of the triangle is whatever is Highest for the one who is meditating —the Object of Supreme Devotion—the Master Pattern of Life. At one of the lower corners is the dedicated personality of the meditator. At the other lower corner is the subject of meditation— the problem to be solved, the friend who needs help, the talk which must be prepared, the hatred which must be turned into co-operation, the committee project which must be brought out of chaos into creativity. Meditation consists in holding the two lower corners of the triangle in relation to each other, in the presence and under the power of the Supreme, until a living pattern of action unites them. . . .

In our hurry to get at the problem in hand, we are prone to forget the invocation of the Highest. If we fail to invoke it, we either get no solution, or we reach a makeshift adjustment between the two lower corners of the triangle, without fitting into the Master Pattern.[2]

This is a very simple and practical form which every one of us should learn to use habitually. It is very human, growing directly out of some life situation. It is, therefore, very real to us. Whenever we find ourselves confronting a problem which we need to solve, or a situation which we need to meet, or a personal relationship which disturbs us, let us not react to it merely on the human level with our own unaided powers. Let us pray about it. But in prayer let us not pray in a horizontal relationship involving merely ourselves and our prob-

[2] New York: Abingdon Press, 1937, pp. 36-37.

lem. Let us rather begin a meditative form of prayer. Let us decide upon some one attribute of God which answers to our life-situation. If we are confronting a situation which is greater than we can meet, let us think of God's power. If we are disturbed in our relations with people, let us consider God's love. If life has become tangled and our nerves are tense, let us think of God's peace. If we are tempted, let us think of the holiness of God or of His redemptive passion in Christ. Let us take any of the great thoughts about God and make this the object of our meditation.

Our first act, then, is to turn away from our problem, to lift ourselves up the side of the triangle that slopes from us toward God. We grow quiet, become reverent in His Presence, fill our minds and hearts with an attempt to apprehend the living reality of that attribute of God on which we are meditating. In a word, we first make this real prayer by making it God-centered. Then we look from the height of this experience down the other side of the triangle at our problem or at the person involved. We try to see him as God sees him, to feel toward him as Christ feels toward him. Perhaps our hot personal resentments may dissolve in understanding, and we may come to share Christ's everlasting pity over one who has been made a disagreeable and aggressive personality through some background of circumstance of which we have not hitherto been aware. Or again, we look down on some problem that had seemed too great for us to handle, but which we now face with the consciousness of God's power to deal with it.

Finally we come back to the base line of the triangle. But something has happened to it in this process. By the upward pull of God upon our souls we have been lifted away from our corner of the triangle. The person or the problem at the other corner has likewise been drawn upward, by the tug of the Eternal, away from the earth plane. The lines of spiritual force now meet somewhere in the center of the triangle. A new and transformed situation begins to emerge. We have arrived at a new method of approach and have been led to perceive new possibilities of solution and action. Problems that cannot be solved while they remain on the earth plane can now be conquered. There are no blank walls in God's universe. There is a way out of every situation, but sometimes both we and our problems must first be lifted Godward to a new level. Such meditative prayer as this surely can become a normal and effective part of the devotional life of every one of us.

One way of keeping meditation vital is thus to take a life situation with us into the holy place of prayer. As a matter of fact, we cannot escape life anyhow. Perhaps this is one of the deep roots of the distractions that sometimes plague us in prayer. Down below the threshold of present attention crouch the worries that have beset us. Pushed down to some cellar of shame are the sins of which we are all too guiltily conscious. Clamoring for attention are the unsolved problems which we face. Gnawing at our vitals are the fears and anxieties that surround us. Churning within us are the tensions of unresolved conflicts. Smoldering like banked fires are the resentments and irritations of repressed angers. Sapping our vitality is a haunting sense of our inadequacy to grapple with some unavoidable task that lies before us. Of what avail is it then to go through forms of prayers, to utter exalted phrases, and to meditate upon the highest while this inner mass of unsolved problems disturbs us?

As a matter of plain fact, we cannot escape our real problems. If we try, they erupt in distracting thoughts that break through our attempted concentration in prayer. But these wandering thoughts should not be treated as a disturbance. They should be welcomed as a call to such reality in prayer as shall lift them into the solving and creative consciousness of the Presence of Him who can invincibly answer life's every need. Here prayer discovers a motivation that is inescapable. Our need to be saved from these unsatisfactory states impels us with utmost urgency and reality to seek the Divine Saviour who can deliver us. This is a living experience daily available for every child of God.

CHAPTER XI

God-Centered Prayer

MENTAL PRAYER—ITS MAJOR FORMS

My meditation of him shall be sweet: I will be glad in the Lord.
—Ps. 104:34

FAMILIARITY WITH THE ENRICHING FORMS OF MENTAL PRAYER that have been used by Christian leaders down through the centuries will aid us in making our prayer-life more God-centered. By their use we shall be helped to practice the art of meditation and learn the rewarding joys that come from brooding upon the attributes of God, considering vital spiritual truths, and meditating upon the life of our Master.

1. THE CLASSIC METHOD

Back in the 1530's Ignatius of Loyola developed a set of spiritual exercises designed to reinstate Jesus on the throne of the heart and to establish an attachment to Him that could never be broken. These exercises have been influential through the centuries as a pattern for similar devotional practices that have been gradually developed. In an effort to gather up the essentials of the classic method and its various developments, I have tried to analyze the five essential parts which recur in nearly all of them. There is an innumerable company of saintly men and women who have found profit in this form of meditation. It should therefore be familiar to every one of us, and we should seek to make this method a normal part of our prayer experience.

The Forward Movement Commission of the Protestant Episcopal Church has suggested five appropriate names for these steps which because of their alliteration can easily be remembered: prepare, picture, ponder, promise, pray.[1]

a. Prepare. Our remote preparation comes from the background of sincere Christian living from which all real prayer must rise. We must never forget that we are constantly preparing for prayer by the way we live our daily lives.

Our *proximate preparation* begins the night before. In our vesper prayer period we read our Bible in accordance with some planned sequence, and then select a verse or a phrase as the subject on which we are to meditate the next morning. Any incident or teaching in the life of Christ might be chosen. Or we might for a period center our attention upon the attributes of God and arrange our scripture reading to center about these. Again, we might study the great Christian virtues, or, by contrast, the seven deadly sins, which are: lust, anger, gluttony, covetousness, envy, sloth, and pride. Our topics for meditation might follow through the Apostles' Creed, the Lord's Prayer, the Beatitudes, the Ten Commandments, or any other topics of spiritual interest.

Thus we combine regular Bible reading with ordered prayer. We learn to read devotionally in preparation for adjusting our lives to God. We select that phrase or verse from our reading which seems to have some insistent message for us. We write it upon a card or memorize it. We think about it and perhaps select certain points for our later consideration. And then we add to our devotional preparation some study that will give us as rich a background as possible to aid us in opening up new meanings which we have never seen in the passage before.

We now come to our *immediate preparation.* Our meditation will naturally occupy our major devotional period, which, as we have suggested, should be wherever possible in the morning hours. Our initial act upon awakening should be to lift our hearts toward God in some act of reverent adoration. While

[1] *We Can Pray,* p. 32.

we are dressing, we should strive to point our minds forward to the coming of the prayer period.

When the time for meditation comes, we seek immediately to place ourselves consciously in the Presence of God, using four acts of devotion as suggested in the discussion of vocal prayer. We may pause to offer our act of stillness a step or two before we arrive at our place of prayer. We consider what we are going to do and ask, "Whither am I moving and for what purpose?" We let the mind repose a little until we grow silent, considering how God is looking at us and inviting us into the secret place of the Most High.

As we offer our act of recollection, we center our hearts on God. We feel "that we are kneeling before a great Personality without form but having an intensely personal love which surrounds us." [2] This should be for us a fact of conviction even before it is a fact of consciousness. Prayer is rooted in the strength of our faith, not in the intensity of our feelings. If we believe that God is omnipresent, and that He is love, and that His Spirit dwells within us, we should affirm with reality of faith that God is with us when we pray. That we may realize this, we offer some act such as the following: "O my heart, my heart, truly God is here," or, "O my God, I believe that Thou art here present, and I adore Thee from the depths of my heart."

Next we offer an act of confession. Instinctively we sense our unworthiness to kneel in the Presence of God. We evidence the sincerity of our desire to commune with Him by expressing penitence for all sins that disturb our relationship to Him.

Then follows an act of invocation in which we ask God to help us as we pray. We offer to Him our minds, our affections, our wills. We ask grace to deepen our spiritual attention. We petition the Holy Spirit to guide us into truth by repeating such a prayer as that contained in the hymn:

[2] L. E. Cox, *The Way in Prayer* (London: A. R. Mowbray & Co., Ltd., 1932), p. 36.

Spirit of God, descend upon my heart;
Wean it from earth; through all its pulses move;
Stoop to my weakness, mighty as Thou art,
And make me love Thee as I ought to love.[8]

b. Picture. We now use our memory to recall the subject which we are to consider, and set it before us with the aid of our imagination. We should not fear to use our imagination with sincerity and confidence. There is a distinction that should be clearly recognized between fancy and creative imagination. Fancy is the power to picture something regardless of whether or not it is true. Fanciful conjectures are rightly suspect. Creative imagination, on the other hand, enables us to picture vividly and vitally something known, on other grounds, to be true. It is one of our highest and most creative faculties. Discoveries, inventions, poetry, music, fruitful scientific hypotheses, and profound philosophical insights have grown out of man's power of creative imagination. Its use in meditation will make the truth considered come alive for us, will grip our attention, stimulate our minds to think, and prepare our hearts and wills for active response. Until we picture our conceptions, they remain vague and have only a feeble power to energize our wills.

The failure to use our imaginations in prayer is one cause for distractions. We are natively picture-minded. If we try to disregard imagination, the vividness of its power may flash disturbing visions around the margins of our thought. In meditation we are seeking to learn to concentrate, to control our attention, to direct our minds into spiritual channels. We therefore decide to spread before our minds the pictures at which we voluntarily desire to look. We thus take one more step in the spiritual focusing of our personalities upon God.

The most direct way by which we may picture our subject is through *imaginative representation.* We have grown so familiar with Bible passages that all too often they are only black words on white paper. If we try to call up the scene

[8] George Croly.

135

before our minds, it is all a neutral gray. We now try to re-capture the full actuality of some event by successively asking: What do we see? What do we hear? What are the people doing and saying? We may even call in the other senses of taste, smell, and touch.

For instance, suppose that the Twenty-third Psalm has furnished the background for our meditation. When we ask, "What do we see?" we might answer, "A shepherd," but this may be for us only a word or an abstract idea. We must press further, asking, "What color is his face? His hair? His garments? What is the expression on his face as he looks toward the sheep? Does he speak and call to them? And the sheep—are they stationary or moving? What color are they against the background? And there is grass there. Do we see its greenness? And the reds and yellows and blues of the flowers? Do we think merely of abstract hills, or do they become more real to us as brown rocks boldly outcropping amid the olive green of the vegetation? Do we hear the rush and gurgle of the water, the wind in the trees, and the bird songs at evening, perchance the shepherd's pipe with its plaintive melody? Do we actually pass through the valley filled with the purpling and mysterious shadows of approaching night? Do we see the stream broadening into a pool of still waters which catch the liquid reflections of trees and sheep and shepherd and hills and sky?" And so we go on, painting in the living reality of the background. How much more awake our minds will be to interpret the truth of some verse of this psalm when it is thus imaginatively re-created in full reality before our minds.

Many subjects cannot be pictured as definitely as the Twenty-third Psalm. Increasing practice, however, will en-able us to use the power of creative imagination in connection with almost any subject being considered. If we should be meditating upon the Sermon on the Mount, we could readily picture the scene, and the people with their varied interests and responses. We could hear the voice of Christ as he spoke the words upon which we meditate. Surely it is always a kindling experience to picture Christ in his divine humanity. Our adoration and response grow deeper as we contemplate the full wonder of His incarnate life.

When we are considering such abstract subjects as the attributes of God we can make use of stimulating *illustrations*. For example, when we meditate upon the divine omnipotence we might picture God's power in the granite upthrust of great mountains or the awesome surge of the sea. The prophets used such devices to make their truths vivid, and Jesus continually turned to concrete pictures and parables to make His revelations of eternal truth more real. Yet another way in which we can make our subjects real to ourselves is by recalling examples in our own experience when God has led us beside the still waters or when some friend has had a definite experience of God's shepherding care. Relating truth to personal experience brings to it warmth and vitality.

Another method for picturing our subject is *interior presentation*. We consider the event as though the action were being performed in our presence. For instance, our souls may be brought in their solitude into direct imaginative contact with the mysteries of the life of Christ.

To stand in the very presence of Christ crucified powerfully moves us to an understanding of His redemptive work. Reverently to enter the Upper Room where once Christ came to stand a Living Presence in the midst of His disciples on Easter evening and to hear him say, "Peace be unto you: as my Father hath sent me, even so send I you" (John 20:21), might quicken us to a profound sharing of this experience until we became conscious here and now that the place of our meditation is the Upper Room of His eternal Presence. The emphasis in this form of imaginative picturing is in vivifying the event as a part of our own personal experience, considering it as if we were right there.

Very frequently our interest in some subject is so immediate and personal that it is not necessary to use the step of imaginative picturing in our meditation. This is true when the subject is one in which we are personally implicated, as in self-examination, or meditation on the existence of God and our personal relationship to Him. But always we should pause to realize the truth profoundly and vividly before we proceed to its consideration.

We do not expect to find ultimate spiritual reality in terms of sensory images. We use them as a starting point to enable us to go beyond them. In the rest of life we begin with sense experience and then go on to the laws and the realities that lie behind it. Similarly in meditation we start with imagination, but we know that later in our pilgrimage we shall outgrow this practice and pass into a more immediate apprehension of spiritual reality.

c. Ponder. Having set the scene vividly before us until it begins to glow with life and meaning, we now turn the full power of our thought upon it, asking that it yield to us its meaning.

There are many methods to help us think in a sustained and penetrating way about the spiritual truths implicit in the subject we are considering. We can prod our minds with questions, asking, Who? Where? Why? How? When? For whom? By what aids? With what love? With what fruit? A very simple method is to consider each significant word or phrase in a chosen scripture verse, staying with it until it yields its deeper and less obvious meaning. We should strive to break through our accustomed stereotypes until fresh insights begin to emerge.

Perhaps the most normal way of proceeding with our consideration is by dividing the subject into two or three main points and then in turn striving to define, describe, or illustrate each of them. (We must be careful to pray about these and not merely to sermonize about them.) Again, we can develop the subject by sheer logic: stating certain premises and drawing their conclusions, searching out fallacies, seeking for abiding principles and eternal truths, and then deducing their corollaries for our faith and our lives. Or we might proceed to turn three powers of our mind upon the subject. As we turn our memory upon it, we ask, What do I know about it? As we employ our intellect, we ask, What do I think of it? As we consider its relation to our will, we query, What can I do about it?

We must strive at all times to keep our thinking dynamic. The object of the meditation is never mere speculation, far less intellectual gymnastics. This is a firsthand encounter with Reality. When we are at prayer, we should frequently lift short petitions for God to help us by revealing His truth and His will. God should frequently be addressed with words of recall so that we are constantly aware that we are brooding in His Presence, guided by His Spirit. We are investigating and considering because we seek to know God's intention for our own lives and His relationship to us. Our meditation will therefore frequently be facing such questions as these: What in respect to this have I done hitherto? What shall I do from today? What obstacles shall I encounter? What means must I take? We ask: What does this truth mean to me? What message from God does this scene bear? Sometimes it is well for us to keep in mind a particular virtue of which we stand in need and to seek light as to how others have achieved it or as to how God can help us to attain this victory. An abiding motivation is found for our pondering when we continually relate it to our lives.

Ultimately we are seeking to know God at first hand. We are stretching the mind to grasp the overpowering reality of God and His larger purposes for life and the Kingdom. We are not called to think great thoughts about God, but only to pay loving attention to Him. We are training our minds to constant and peaceful attention to God and ceaseless subordination to His will. As we thus ponder about some vital truth, life deepens into real communion with God. Then we humbly wait, as in His Presence, for some real insight to be manifested in our hearts. As we gaze at some verse of scripture, out of hundreds of possible meanings one suddenly comes to life. Some message comes to our hearts with such unexpected life and force as clearly evidences the inspiring action of the Spirit of God. Our faith becomes more vital. Graciously God reveals to us His real nature, His holy will, and His suffering love.

Centuries ago a priest in an ancient Egyptian temple wrote upon one of the walls his conception of the deity whom he reverently sought: "I am he that was and is and evermore shall be; and my veil hath no man lifted." A later priest inscribed upon the opposite wall these words: "Veil after veil have I lifted, and ever the face grows more wonderful." This is our sublime privilege at the height of meditation.

d. Promise. As we ponder upon the deep things of God and appreciate His grace and His love, we sense a stirring of something in the very heart of us which instinctively is responding to His presence. "Deep calleth unto deep." As we come to know God more clearly and more personally in our meditation, we sense that the adjustment of our relationship to Him is the central demand of life. If we truly know Him, we must sincerely follow Him. We meditate in order that we may "purify our souls, amend our ways, guard against temptation, and strengthen our purposes." We gaze upon God that the profoundest emotions within us may be stirred and that our wills may be moved toward oneness with His holy, wise, and loving will.

Throughout our meditation acts of will should already have been interspersed. After some picture quickens our thoughts, we glimpse the meaning of the scene for our lives and swiftly promise God to live anew upon this higher plane. As we ponder and deepen in our searching until we come into the very Presence of God, we swiftly respond to calls as they are inspoken in our worshiping hearts.

But every meditation should, near its conclusion, come to a definite period in which our promises are specifically framed. One of the great laws of the inner life is this: no prayer is true prayer until it issues in an act of response. Until our wills carry over into life some intention to carry out God's will or to abide in some new relationship to Him, we have not reached that depth of sincerity which lies close to the heart of real praying. Prayer is not a golden glow or a purple mood. It is the achievement of such a oneness with the Spirit of God as impels us at any cost to adjust our daily living to the level of His high purposes for us and to clear from our consciousness every hidden barrier that impedes the flow of God's power through us. To this end we now make a series of resolutions through which we express the promises we feel led to make.

First, there should be a *general resolution* to give ourselves entirely to God in all things today. We offer up our memories, our imaginations, our thoughts, our affections, and our wills to be entirely God's throughout the day. We realize that the only power that can enable us to achieve this resolution is the strong grace of our Lord and Saviour Jesus Christ. With a profound distrust of ourselves, but with utter confidence in Him, we make this general oblation of our lives.

A second general resolution which might well be made is to avoid all sin today. We are conscious of how often we have fallen. With renewed intensity we add a petition to our resolution, "Our Father which art in heaven, deliver us from evil."

But the climax of the promises which we make comes in one or more *definite resolutions*. These should be as particular as we can possibly make them. It is so easy to make a general promise or an abstract intention. Suppose that instead, then, we make the first resolution that comes spontaneously into the center of our consciousness. The Spirit of God has stimulated us to turn our attention to an area where advance is called for. But we must not stop with this initial phrasing. We must meditate for a moment until we can make it still sharper; then try yet again, making it as concrete and specific as possible. We need not try always to promise some great thing. It is the lesser virtues which help us to attain the greater ones. We can pray about such humble habits and actions as keeping our tongue, performing some humble act for one of God's children, or avoiding a nagging spirit. But we must make our promise definite, something to be done today, even at a particular time. This will enable us the better to check back on the accomplishment of our resolution, and will keep us from getting lost in clouds of unreal and largely meaningless generalities. The following resolutions may serve to suggest the type of promises which many have found most effective:

Solemnly to hand over to God's keeping one small fear.
An attempt to make one half-hour of work during the day a special vehicle for God's power.
To endeavour to pass a whole day without making an excuse.
To get through the day without a grumble.
Intentionally to copy one of Christ's actions during the day.[4]

e. Pray. As we meditate, our whole personality should become more and more centered in God. The very object of this method is to make a transition from self-centered to God-centered prayer; in a word, to become more recollected. Throughout the meditation, brief spontaneous prayers will have been offered. The whole experience is carried on increasingly in the consciousness of God's Presence guiding us into all truth and leading us into deeper life. Words of recall—usually one of the names of God—brief ejaculations, and sincere aspirations are native to all parts of meditation. But there should always come a time when we slowly shift our gaze from the subject considered to God, by whose grace we have been meditating. We pass into a spontaneous form of prayer, informal and intimate—the colloquy—which is the normal way of praying for all of us. This free conversation with God is now, however, carried forward upon a new level where all of our powers are keenly awake and where our communion with the Eternal Father moves upon a new and more kindling spiritual plane.

Our colloquy is free and unplanned. Petitions are offered. We ask grace to put into practice our promises and to keep our resolutions. We seek victory over temptation, especially our ruling temptation. We ask for a particular grace which has been central in our pondering. We ask for "personal

[4] L. E. Cox, *The Way in Prayer*, pp. 7-8.

interior knowledge of our Lord that we may love Him more dearly and follow Him more nearly." We voice our desire for a closer union with God. But what will unite us to God? Not merely our good thoughts but the good movement of our wills and affections is needed. We offer up intercession for many others. We use acts of devotion that rise unbidden from our hearts to express our praise, love, homage, and faith.

This basic method of prayer, which we have centered around five key words—prepare, picture, ponder, promise, and pray—we now have before us. Only the briefest and most essential suggestions have been made for each aspect, yet the newness of this method to many of us and the multiplicity of counsels may even now seem confusing. But let us persevere in coming back to these suggestions again and again, for they represent the combined wisdom of the great masters of prayer in all ages. Each day one of the five emphases might be made central until we feel more at home in its use, then another and another until at last we discipline our minds and bring every power of our personalities readily to bear upon some great theme which leads us at last to the majestic reality of the Presence of God.

Wondrously, as we continue, there may come to us a slow but ceaseless revelation of God through prayer.

2. AFFECTIVE PRAYER

As we practice the art of mental prayer, there will come times when our hearts will be drawn directly toward God. Feelings will surge up out of the deeps of us in response to Him whom we have glimpsed in our meditation. Fired by the love of God, we shall then leave our considerations and our methods and respond in spontaneous and fervent outpourings of adoration, praise, and love.

This experience is known as affective prayer. The word "affective" refers to the predominance of the affective or feeling side of our consciousness in this outreach to God. It is a form of meditation, differing from it only in degree. In it we apprehend truth more directly. Brooding thought is not absent, but our affections are more numerous and more varied. It is far removed from sentimentalism. It lives in the realm of the truest emotions that stir the human heart. It arises out of our appreciation of life's highest values and supreme certainties. Only these rich emotions can mature that adoration of God which is the very top note of the human spirit. This form of meditation is the transition to the first stage of contemplation, in which we rise toward the very Presence of the eternal God.

An alternative name for this experience of affective prayer is the Prayer of the Heart. Frequently as we are praying, God will become real in our thinking. His Presence will seem to be very near. In a direct and immediate way our hearts reach out toward Him. We break into a conversational prayer or brief acts of devotion which now are intensified and more expressive of the depth of our worship. Every one of us is familiar with this more intimate pouring out of our souls toward the Almighty Friend who has drawn graciously near to us as we prayed. Whenever we feel our hearts moved toward this type of prayer, we should leave off our considerations and let our spirits reach out toward God in this meaningful experience of devotion.

3. THE SULPICIAN METHOD

The Sulpician Method is a form of meditation developed in the seventeenth century in the seminary of St. Sulpice in Paris by the Oratorian Fathers de Bérulle, Olier, and de Condren. It is a simple and beautiful method of Christ-centered prayer. In it there is an intermingling of the classical form of meditation and affective prayer. It verges on contemplation and may, in fact, pass into that higher stage of our pilgrimage from self to God. We prepare ourselves, as in ordinary meditation, by placing ourselves consciously in the Presence of God. But we realize that it is through Jesus Christ our Lord that we can most directly approach the Heavenly Father. We recognize that in the life of Jesus there are both historical actions and eternal states. The birth of our Lord is an act taking place at a certain moment and at a particular location, but the Incarnation is a permanent state that abides in time as in eternity. The Son of God is eternally given to men. Again, Calvary is an act taking place there and then, but how much more is it a state having a permanent, eternal character! In our prayer we are to seek contact with the Living Christ in whom there lives eternally all that we meditate upon in His earthly life. Inspired by these convictions, we enter upon the three stages of this method of meditation:

a. Christ Before My Eyes: Adoration. We first consider and look upon Jesus Christ in love and reverence. He is so holy, so divine. We select one of His actions for our consideration. But then we think of this in its eternal setting, and ask Christ to reveal to us its meaning now. The spirit of the emphasis in this method is the same as that suggested by Teresa in the preceding century when she said:

As you are alone, seek for some companion—and where could you find a better one than the Master? Picture this same Lord close beside you. See how lovingly, humbly He is teaching you . . . practice it, practice it! I am not now asking you to meditate upon Him, nor to produce great thoughts, nor to feel deep devotion; I only ask you to look at Him.[5]

Then we feel the call to put on the mind of Christ, to know His desires and His will. We see the Christian virtues, not as abstractions but as they are in Him. We are not called to imitate Him as a model, but to possess His life within us and to feel Him inspire the birth of His virtues in our lives. We are called to leave our self-centeredness and to cleave to Christ. We are called by His voice to a twofold response: Deny thyself, and follow me.

b. Christ in My Heart: Communion. We are called in our first act of this meditation to adore Christ, in the second to love Him. Our hearts are to be united with Him. Our considerations lead us to a fervent desire to be united in some

[5] *Life,* IX. 4.

145

virtue that lives in Him. We therefore ask for His spirit. We ask Him to make in us a new heart. We have been looking at Him in order that we may be conformed to Him.

> Take time to be holy,
>   The world rushes on;
> Spend much time in secret
>   With Jesus alone;
> By looking to Jesus,
>   Like Him thou shalt be;
> Thy friends in thy conduct
>   His likeness shall see.[6]

As we thus invite Him into our hearts, we are aware of our need for repentance. We see our need for the virtue which we have been considering. We are aware of our failings. We desire to escape from our lukewarmness. We want to rise to real communion with His Spirit. We therefore are moved to lift our petition that God will give us the grace of achieving this Christlikeness of heart. Our sincere prayer now is: "Grow Thou, O Christ, in me!"

c. Christ in My Hands: Co-operation. We now desire to co-operate with the grace that has been manifested to us in our prayer. Our wills are united with His will. We desire that nothing should act in us save Christ. We want Him to do through us all that He desires to do. We sincerely desire to reproduce the life of Jesus. "The Christian wants to adhere to Christ, abide in Christ, live with Christ." We therefore make our resolutions to live in the future in conformity with the light which we have received in prayer. We resolve that we will practice the same day the virtue which we have considered. We associate that resolution with some loving aspiration which we repeat often during the course of the day. This is similar to the thought of Francis de Sales, who suggests that we conclude any meditation with what he calls a "spiritual nosegay."

[6] William D. Longstaff.

As when we walk about a beautiful garden we desire to carry away a few flowers and enjoy their perfume, so we should gather one or two points from our meditation "in which we have found most relish and which are most proper for our advancement," so as to recall and act upon them during the day.[7]

Thus to dwell on Christ is "an admirable and beautiful kind of prayer." Its three points of adoration, communion, and co-operation parallel the first three points in the Lord's Prayer. How better could we make prayer real than by meditating frequently in this threefold sequence: Christ before my eyes, Christ in my heart, Christ in my hands?

[7] *Introduction to the Devout Life* (London: Burns, Oates & Washbourne, Ltd., 1934), pp. 63-64.

CHAPTER XII

Life-Changing Spiritual Exercises

MENTAL PRAYER—ITS CHARACTER TEST

Blessed are the pure in heart: for they shall see God.
—Matt. 5:8

IT IS A SIGNIFICANT FACT THAT WHENEVER ANYONE CAME SEEK-
ing to understand the higher realms of the spiritual life, Jesus
always confronted him with a moral demand. The rich young
ruler came asking, "Good Master, what shall I do to inherit
eternal life?" Immediately Jesus saw the point of moral failure
in his life. His soul was entrapped in his possessions. The way
to eternal life for him was in letting go of these earthly entan-
glements. He must face a reorganization of his whole world of
values through response to the Master's call: "Sell that thou
hast, and give to the poor." (Matt. 19:21.)

When the woman of Samaria, talking with Jesus by the well
near Sychar, inquired about the water of life, He cut across
her superficial discussion with a command that struck the heart
of her moral failure: "Go, call thy husband and come hither."
(John 4:16.) When Nicodemus came to Jesus by night to
talk with Him as a teacher come from God and to search for
the power behind the miracles which He wrought, he was
confronted with the words, "Verily, verily, I say unto thee,
Except a man be born again, he cannot see the kingdom of
God." (John 3:5.)

The first demand in prayer is a sincere moral response to
God. There is a character test in prayer. The quality of our
living determines the quality of our praying. The psalmist

148

said, "If I regard iniquity in my heart, the Lord will not hear me" (Ps. 66:18), and Jesus phrased the positive facet of this truth in the Beatitude in His Sermon on the Mount: "Blessed are the pure in heart: for they shall see God."

This is inevitably true. Even our earliest and most elementary experiences of God bring with them this insistent and inescapable demand to bring our lives into harmony with His will. Conversion marks a pivotal point in our spiritual life. Then, after that, at every stage of our upward progress in prayer there is a corresponding deepening of the divine demand for our loyalty and devotion. A life process accompanies and parallels the prayer process at every point.

If we would seek to know God in prayer, therefore, we must begin by purgation. Spiritual exercises following the classic method of meditation offer a most effective means for this process of adjusting our lives to His will. Let us become thoroughly acquainted with the application of this method by observing in detail the outline of a planned succession of meditations that may enable us to know God more profoundly, to see ourselves more honestly, to look at Christ more devotedly, and to consider our future pathway more earnestly. We shall survey the exercises now with two purposes in mind: (1) to see a concrete illustration of how to proceed with a personal spiritual retreat of four weeks of meditative devotion that can be life-changing in its cumulative effect; and (2) to discover through definite examples how we may develop meditative material of our own throughout the rest of our lives.

FIRST WEEK: DEEPENING OUR KNOWLEDGE OF GOD

If we would really know and grapple with our sin, we must first see God through reverent prayer and profound meditation. The motivating dynamic of our soul-purification is some arresting vision of God. We therefore begin the process of purgation by reflecting upon the central truths of our faith.

Let us view the complete process for the first day, using the five steps with alliterative names suggested in the preceding chapter, and then briefly note the topics that may guide our meditations for the remaining days of the week.

First Day: Basic Grounds for Our Belief in God. To prepare, we begin the night before in our devotional reading, which may be the eleventh chapter of Hebrews, from which we choose for special thought the verse: "He that cometh to God must believe that he is, and that he is a rewarder of them that diligently seek him." (Heb. 11:6.) Then in the morning our immediate preparation is to place ourselves consciously in the Presence of God by offering four acts of devotion: stillness, in which we turn to God in quiet confidence; recollection, in which we reverently and worshipfully center our attention on God; confession, in which we search our hearts that there may be utter sincerity in our search for God; invocation, in which we ask God's Spirit to be graciously near us, to help us as we pray, and to lead us into deeper truth.

Since our concern is so present and so vivid, we may omit the step of picturing and go directly to our pondering, in which we consider the subject of our meditation profoundly and prayerfully.

First, we may ponder the general or philosophical grounds for our belief in God. Is our faith rooted in reason? What kind of universe do we live in? Is it a great machine, grinding on through the ages, blank as to purpose and void of all meaning and value? Is it a soulless swirl of atoms? If this is our view, then what of our lives ultimately? Where do we come from? Is it all a vast mystery before our creation, and a black tragedy after our death? What a difference if we can honestly say, "I believe in God the Father Almighty"! Let us grapple profoundly with these thoughts until we struggle through to a living faith for ourselves and convincing reasons for it. These are urgent questions. We cannot dodge them permanently. Our very destiny is involved in our answers. As we meditate prayerfully, God graciously brings into the focus of our thinking new insights into our essential faith and powerful convictions in the assurance of which we can henceforth live.

Second, we may ponder our Christian knowledge of God. What have others discovered about Him? Is our faith rooted in revelation? What have the greatest spiritual prophets of the ages found? Supremely, what have we found of God in Jesus Christ? The greatest fact in the spiritual history of mankind was our Master's consciousness of God. Uniquely God was in Him to reconcile the world to Himself, to bridge the chasm between man and God, and to reveal the very nature of God's heart. Have we "beheld the glory of God in the face of Jesus Christ"? How pivotal He is for our lives! Without Him we grope in the dark with only the feeble flicker of our own insights to illumine the ultimate way. What if we discover in Christ the very reality of God visiting humanity to reveal Himself to us! What if His hands pushed back the great curtains of the beyond and gave the deathless certainty of life going on eternally through God's grace! Then how central our relationship to Christ, how vital that we should come to know Him whom we have believed!

Finally, we should ponder our personal knowledge of God. What do we know about Him at first hand? Is our faith rooted in experience? How real is our life of prayer? How near is God to us now? Are we dwelling in the secret place of the Most High? Can we now hear Him saying within us, "Be still, and know that I am God"?

This can be for us not merely a meditation but a life-changing spiritual exercise. We are, with utter honesty, wrestling with the very structure of our souls in the presence of God. As, after this soul-searching period, we come to the time of promise, our resolutions will be unusually pointed and real. We promise that we will more often stop to recall the real "frame of reference" in which we live, to become aware that we cannot continue to exist for a single moment except as God wills and upholds our existence. Our relation to Him is paramount. What is His will for us now? Have we been indifferent, lukewarm, heedless, blinded by secular concerns, engrossed in the pursuit of transient values that shall pass away? Has prayer as our living relationship to God been central in our daily program? As we thus meditate, let us determine upon and offer to God now our new spiritual resolutions.

Finally, as we pray, we pour out our hearts in thanksgiving for God's upholding care, in consecration to His purposes for us, and in petition for Him to uphold us in our new resolves.

Similarly, we may proceed to work out for ourselves a meditation for each of the remaining days of the week on the basis of the key thoughts suggested in the following paragraphs.

Second Day: The Divine Nature. We think of Isaiah's vision of the Lord, high and lifted up, with His glory filling the temple, and the seraphim crying one unto another, "Holy, holy, holy, is the Lord of hosts: the whole earth is full of his glory." (Isa. 6:1-3.) God is so far beyond our thinking that we are overwhelmed by the ultimate mystery of His being. We meditate upon His august words: "I am that I am." He only is absolute, "one set apart, incomparable, unapproachable, sublime." Before His lofty exaltation, we see our creaturehood. We are dependent utterly on the divine upholding. Man apart from God is nothing.

Third Day: God's Omnipresence. The boundlessness of space overwhelms us. Our two-hundred-inch telescope reveals its cold, awesome depths stretching out through the unthinkable distance of a billion light years. Yet God holds it in the hollow of His mighty hand. It is His universe; everywhere in it He is present, ceaselessly energizing it in accordance with His creative will. He it is who encompasses and pervades our being. "Whither shall I go from thy spirit? or whither shall I flee from thy presence?" (Ps. 139:7.)

Fourth Day: God's Eternity. Time stretches back through the incomprehensible aeons of the past and forward into an unending future, and through it all God eternally exists. "Before the mountains were brought forth, or ever thou hadst formed the earth and the world, even from everlasting to everlasting, thou art God." (Ps. 90:2.) We see our own lives, finite and limited and approaching an inevitable end in this world. Then do we "fall sheer a blinded thing" into nothingness, or are we grasped and upheld by the hand of Eternal Love and through His grace made partakers of eternal life? How such a meditation detaches us from all things that do not last, saying, "This, too, shall pass!"

Fifth Day: God's Unchangeability. We consider the prophet's words: "The grass withereth, the flower fadeth: but the word of our God shall stand forever." (Isa. 40:8.) The dependability of the stars and the forces that operate harmoniously throughout the boundlessness of space and time are rooted in His ageless purposes. The character of God holds our universe steady. We too can depend on His unchanging grace. "Thou wilt keep him in perfect peace, whose mind is stayed on thee." (Isa. 26:3.)

> Change and decay in all around I see;
> O thou, who changest not, abide with me.[1]

Only in God is peace found. Only in Him can our hearts find rest.

Sixth Day: God's Perfection. We see the awesome heights of His holiness, the fire of His purity. We sense His unbounded wisdom that comprehends all creation at a glance and "understands our thoughts afar off." We see Him as the mighty Artist of all beauty, the tremendous Mind of all truth, and the animating Soul of all goodness. We gaze on God's perfections and hear with awe the words: "Be ye therefore perfect, even as your Father which is in heaven is perfect." (Matt. 5:48.)

Seventh Day: God's Love. We meditate on the three greatest words ever written: "God is love." (I John 4:16.) We sense that His mighty power is not merely power, but power of love. It is love that beats at the heart of our universe. It is redemptive love. There is a cross forever at the heart of God. There is in the midst of the throne a "Lamb slain from the foundation of the world." In Christ on Calvary we see the amazing depths of a love we shall never fathom. And that love is for us, His

[1] Henry F. Lyte.

children. We can abide in it. We can enjoy it forever. How dare we cause the deepest pain of the passion of His heart through our disloyalty or neglect?

> Love so amazing, so divine,
> Demands my soul, my life, my all.[2]

SECOND WEEK: CLARIFYING OUR KNOWLEDGE OF OURSELVES

In the next week of our meditation we make explicit in our lives the implicit moral and spiritual demands of which we have become disturbingly aware as we have gazed on God.

Our ultimate relation is to Him, and anything that disturbs this must be purged from our hearts. We continue the process of purification by making our general meditations real and personal. We seek to know ourselves with utter honesty. We seek out the causes of our faults and our sins.

Sometimes modern psychologists feel that religion unduly emphasizes our inner sense of guilt and that this results in a morbid preoccupation with self. Nothing could be farther from the fact. Religion does not produce a sense of guilt. It rather reveals the centers of guilt that are already there. The only pathway to healthy-mindedness is to face ourselves and seek, with God's help, deliverance from evils with which we have become entangled and forgiveness for sins which we have committed. To turn aside from these centers which are poisoning our inner life by thrusting them out of consciousness through repression, or using escape mechanisms, cannot truly help.

Again, sometimes people point to the evils of overconscientiousness. Concerning this George S. Stewart points out:

Scrupulosity is a very evil thing. It is one of the devil's devices for withdrawing us from the battle with real sins to preoccupation with ourselves over trifles, a most unhealthy occupation, which hinders real warfare and real work. Christ's spirit is given to enable us to

---

[2] Isaac Watts.

live a normal healthy life, not to make us specialists in pathology, either of our own or of other people's moral diseases.[3]

We are not concerned here with pathological guilt complexes nor with morbid scrupulosity. We do not want to exaggerate our faults; we want to face them. Adjustment to reality is one of the essential characteristics of all healthy-mindedness. The ancient advice of Socrates, "Know thyself," is still our highest wisdom.

It is sound advice for us to make our self-knowledge positive as well as negative. We do not want to see ourselves either under morbid illusions or with presumptuous optimism. Candidly and without false humility we want to discover the good qualities which God has entrusted to us. We would thank Him for every gift that is ours from our parents, from our Christian heritage, and from the measure of strength we have achieved through His grace. These are our talents entrusted to us for His glory. We are to nurture them and by His aid move on toward higher perfection. At the same time we seek to discover and face without self-excuse or evasion of any kind the sins and imperfections which impede our progress and hold us back from God.

Our pride, our egocentricity, our inertia, and our many other faulty dispositions make self-knowledge difficult to obtain. Our inner life is exceedingly complex, and our motivating impulses often are hidden from us. Courage, honesty, and perseverance are required; but, more than all else, the enlightening of our minds and consciences by the inner promptings of the Holy Spirit as we pray. The saints, who prayed courageously, knew the heart of man as few others ever have. It is this self-knowledge which, under God's leading, we now seek.

First Day: General Examination of Conscience. Our objective in this meditation is expressed in the prayer of the psalmist: "Search me, O God, and know my heart: try me, and

---

[3] *The Lower Levels of Prayer* (Nashville: Abingdon-Cokesbury Press, 1939), pp. 99-100.

know my thoughts: and see if there be any wicked way in me, and lead me in the way everlasting." (Ps. 139:23-24.) We make this examination by placing ourselves consciously in God's Presence and then considering the following five points suggested by Ignatius of Loyola:

1. To give thanks to God our Lord for the benefits received.
2. To ask grace to know our sins and cast them out.
3. To ask account of our soul from the hour that we rose up to the present Examen, hour by hour, or period by period; and first as to thoughts, and then as to words, and then as to acts.
4. To ask pardon of God our Lord for the faults.
5. To purpose amendment with His grace.[4]

In preparation for such general examination the meditative reading of available devotional material will often be found helpful. For example, Georgia Harkness says in *Religious Living:*

It is not the grosser sins, such as murder, that we need to think about; it is the subtle sins that get hold of us. If you do not know what you have to repent of, ask yourself these questions:

1. Have I criticized anybody too harshly?
2. Have I spread gossip?
3. Have I lost my temper and said unkind things?
4. Have I been jealous of anybody? Resentful or unforgiving?
5. Have I tried to get possessions or honors that belonged to someone else?
6. Have I tried to enjoy myself in ways harmful to others?
7. Have I misused my body or my personality by over-indulgence in something—smoking, drinking, sex?
8. Have I been lazy or irresponsible about something I ought to do?
9. Have I been dishonest or insincere?
10. Have I had too much self-confidence? Or too little?

[4] *Spiritual Exercises,* tr. Elder Mullan (New York: P. J. Kenedy & Sons, 1914), pp. 30-31.

11. Have I been concerned mainly about myself, my own affairs, my success and my future?

12. Have I been snobbish? Prejudiced by the economic or political attitudes of my group?

13. Have I been indifferent to those less privileged—the poor, the sick, the ignorant, those of other races?

14. Have I been indifferent or irreverent toward God? [5]

Second Day: The Particular Examination. In this exercise we come to grips with our special faults and weaknesses. We "divide and conquer" by concentrating upon them one by one. We must here make a frontal assault upon our besetting sin. We must relentlessly seek out its hidden cause. Like the psalmist, we seek a positive goal: "Create in me a clean heart, O God"; but this failure blocks our way, and we must first pray: "Cleanse me from my sin." (Ps. 51:10, 2.)

The classic method for making this particular examen is, again, given by Ignatius of Loyola. He writes:

The first time is in the morning, immediately on rising, when one ought to propose to guard himself with diligence against that particular sin or defect which he wants to correct and amend.

The second time is after dinner, when one is to ask of God our Lord what one wants, namely, grace to remember how many times he has fallen into that particular sin or defect, and to amend himself in the future. Then let him make the first Examen, asking account of his soul of that particular thing proposed, which he wants to correct and amend. Let him go over hour by hour, or period by period, commencing at the hour he rose, and continuing up to the hour and instant of the present Examen, . . . [and let him record] the times he has fallen into that particular sin or defect. Then let him resolve anew to amend himself up to the second Examen which he will make.

The third time: After supper, the second Examen will be made, in the same way, hour by hour, commencing at the first Examen and continuing up to the present [second] one; . . . [and let him

[5] New York: Association Press, 1937, pp. 40-41. Used by permission.

again note] the times he has fallen into that particular sin or defect.[6]

One does not have to perform the exercise exactly in this way, but each of us could profit by some personal adaptation of the method as God now calls us to purge some hidden fault or sin from our lives.

As an alternative we might use a different form of self-examination. Usually the focal point of failure is all too clearly evident to our moral insight after it has been quickened by prayer. We do not have to search about for the sin. We remember immediately that un-Christlike flash of temper, that moment when selfishness took command of us, or that unkind criticism which we thoughtlessly repeated. Joseph Tissot suggests that this quick moment of self-revealing can be accomplished through what he calls "the Glance." Outlining his procedure, he says:

I ask myself this simple question: "Where is my heart?"—but, at the very moment of putting this question, the answer comes within me. This question causes me to cast a rapid glance into the innermost centre of my being, and I at once see that salient point; I give ear to the tone echoed by my soul, and immediately catch the dominant note. It is an intuitive proceeding, and is quite instantaneous. There is no need for intellectual inquiries, efforts of will, and ransacking the memory; I hear and see. It is a glance. It is simple and rapid. A soul must be quite ignorant of its inner self, and quite unaccustomed to enter into itself, if it does not experience this.[7]

Third Day: Renouncing Our Sins. If we desire to pray, we must renounce sin, for God and sin cannot co-exist. When God enters our hearts at conversion, our love causes us to turn from sin to God. But the process of deliverance from sin is not usually completed at conversion. It takes a moment to be born, but it takes a lifetime to grow. "We cannot become

[6] *Spiritual Exercises*, pp. 21-22.
[7] *The Interior Life* (London: Burns, Oates & Washbourne, Ltd.; Westminster, Maryland: Newman Press) , p. 307. Used by permission.

perfect in a day." Throughout our Christian life we are called to grow in grace and in the knowledge of God.

In our meditation we desire to make clear to ourselves the real nature of sin. Sin is enmity against God. It is the choosing of our wills as over against His will. "It is," says Teresa, "as if we said: 'Lord, I know full well this action displeases you, yet I shall do it none the less. I am not unaware that your eyes see it, I know perfectly well you do not want it, but I will rather follow my bent and fancy than your will.' " [8]

Sin expels God from our souls. We are thus left in a godless universe—alone, alienated, hopeless, and cut off. It is not that God is angry with us in the sense that His will is turned against us. His grace is eternal. In love He suffers as we go on bearing the irrevocable consequences of our sins. It is rather that God's will is contrary to our will. He is moving in the direction determined by His holy wisdom. We are going counter to this direction. We disturb the divine order, and God by His very nature must be against us until we turn in answer to His grace and flow with His holy will. It is in this sense that Isaiah truly speaks for God in saying: "When ye make many prayers, I will not hear. . . . Wash you, make you clean; put away the evil of your doings from before mine eyes." (Isa. 1:15-16.)

Now that we are desirous of entering into communion with God, we are called to fight against sin, to purpose to avoid sin in the future, to resolve not to keep anything in our lives that is displeasing to God. We therefore see the necessity of avoiding the occasions of sin, resisting the allurements of self-indulgence, and subduing our bodies to our spirits.

Fourth Day: Facing Up to Our Failings. In our conversion we have turned against those major sins that separate us from God. There are, however, many lesser sins and shortcomings that drag on the soul's ascent to God. They are the imperfections to which we are most attached. We do not seriously combat them because we do not want to give them up. These

[8] *Way of Perfection*, XLI.

are, in many cases, more dangerous than the greater sins, for these are our real sins with which we are still battling. We want to be pure in heart, but we find that we are still divided. We have been holding something back. When this is so, there is a coolness between us and God. We tend to drift lower. Forbidden appeals gather strength. We find ourselves upon a descending spiritual spiral. We may not be like Judas, but how often we are like Peter in our denials of Christ! In our prayer now we seek to sensitize our hearts that we may restore our lost oneness with God by accepting the prophet's invitation: "Let the wicked forsake his way, and the unrighteous man his thoughts: and let him return unto the Lord, and he will have mercy upon him; and to our God, for he will abundantly pardon."

Fifth Day: Resisting Our Temptations. Because we are not wholly given to God, temptations find a response in us. Long ago it was pointed out how they come to us: first as a suggestion, then as our pleasure, and finally as our consent. Let us meditate upon the temptations of our Master that we may see how He overcame them.

Temptations are the normal lot of man. They are not sins, nor even imperfections. We cannot prevent their coming to us, but with God's help we can and should resist them. We should do this quietly and with poise, not with anger or impatience. We turn to God in prayer; we rest in His peace; we remain "anchored in the will of God." The author of *The Cloud of Unknowing* says, rather quaintly and yet with rare insight, that when any thoughts and stirrings of sin press upon us, getting between us and God, we should "try to look, as it were, over their shoulders, seeking another thing: the which thing is God." [9] What will enable us to conquer them is not our own strength but God's grace. We must seek to forestall them by being alerted concerning our weak points, the occasions that get us into difficulties, and the rash presumption that deceives us as to our own strength. When temptations do arise, we must

[9] London: John M. Watkins, 1946, p. 112.

resist them promptly, energetically, perseveringly, yet humbly. After temptations have passed we will thank God if we have overcome, remembering that "blessed is the man that endureth temptation." (Jas. 1:12.)

Sixth Day: Making Resolutions of Amendment. We have during this week become aware of the nature of sin and of the reality of the fight which we must wage against it. We now see that resolute action is needed if we are to adjust our lives to God's will. It is much better that we do not disturb ourselves about our sins or look at our guilt unless we mean to do something about them. It would be much better to stay in the psychological protection of some shielding escape mechanisms unless we intend to do battle valiantly with all our souls, and with God's help, until we fight through to a victorious reintegration of life on higher levels.

Through our particular examination we have begun to deal with some one of our sins or failures. We must make this as explicit as we can. George S. Stewart says:

There is a general and shamed feeling that yet never quite gets to grips with reality. It does not say "here, and to that person, and then, and in that way I did this thing that I ought not to have done." The result of this is threefold: it hinders a true and full confession to God: it hinders the determined setting out to do what had been left undone: it shuts the door on the realization of full absolution. There is a world of difference between "I have not been true in speech," and "On Friday I exaggerated the story I told about A.B. so as to discredit him." When we make admissions like that to ourselves, then and not till then can we make a real confession to God; and the way is then open for God to tell us what to say or do.[10]

When we have thus clearly seen our sin and confessed it to God, we must take a succession of positive steps to conquer it. Our first act is to *renounce the evil* which we have discovered and confessed. This clinches the whole process. It is not enough merely to face it and even to be forgiven for this one failure.

---

[10] *Lower Levels of Prayer*, pp. 100-101.

As the final test of our sincerity we must renounce forever what has been at last clearly seen as sin. One of our modern psychiatrists, Karen Horney, reinforces the necessity of renunciation as a step toward healthy-mindedness:

Even if we recognize a conflict as such, we must be willing and able to renounce one of the two contradictory issues. But the capacity for clear and conscious renunciation is rare, because our feelings and beliefs are muddled, and perhaps because in the last analysis most people are not secure and happy enough to renounce anything.[11]

The experience of vital contact with God in prayer has so unified our will that we have become secure and integrated enough to desire God's will with all our hearts. Thus we rise above the tension of inner conflict, which sin always produces, and make this primary act of renunciation. Like the prodigal son we say, "I will arise and go to my father." (Luke 15:18.)

Then next we *determine to remake our habits.* Perhaps we have become aware of wrong habits or, it may be, of the absence of certain good habits such as the sacred keeping of our times for prayer. Now, when we have seen these failures, is the time to throw the power of the awakened personality behind a new program. There are two very simple rules by which we can make or break any habit: (1) Begin now. (2) Allow no exceptions. Backed by the power of God with which we have been in contact, we resolve to launch out on some step in life-remaking.

The next act is to *seek ways to mitigate the evil consequences* that have resulted from our failures. Clearly whatever we can do to make restitution for any fault should be done as a first fruit of our real penitence.

Sometimes the only thing that is clear is the next step. We may not know God's entire will for our lives, but for all who sincerely pray there comes a clear intimation of at least one practical step which we can now take. At the climax of prayer

[11] *Our Inner Conflicts* (New York: W. W. Norton & Company, Inc., 1945), p. 26.

we courageously *resolve to take the next step*. Through a definite act of the will we make our resolution.

Seventh Day: Receiving the Forgiving Grace of God. God is taking hold of our lives and remaking them. Apart from Him, we have been chained with habit. Sin has involved us in irrevocable consequences. It has disturbed the subconscious depths of our being with a sense of inescapable guilt and a resultant feeling of anxiety. It has set up an endless torment of inner tensions, but now we see our transgressions caught hold of by the grace and omnipotence of God. We feel Him shattering the chains of habit that have bound us, guiding us to some pathway that will alleviate the consequences of our wrongdoing, releasing us from guilt by forgiveness, and bridging our estrangements from Himself through His redeeming love. This is a spiritual process which is accomplished when we open our souls to God in the sincerity of soul-searching prayer. "If we confess our sins, he is faithful and just to forgive us our sins, and to cleanse us from all unrighteousness." (I John 1:9.) At last we grasp the great reality that God who created us out of nothingness has power to re-create and remake us through the redeeming power of Christ and the active operation of His Holy Spirit within our hearts now.

THIRD WEEK: ENRICHING OUR KNOWLEDGE OF CHRIST

In our third week our endeavor will be to meditate upon our Lord and Saviour Jesus Christ. Our object is to reinstate Jesus on the throne of our heart. We want to establish an attachment to Him which nothing can shake. No finer method of doing this can be found than the use of the Sulpician Method. In our struggle for inner purification we would strive to put on the mind of Christ and to possess His life within us. The virtues which we seek live in Him, and our desire is for Christlikeness of heart. We are aware of how far short we have come of our high calling in Christ Jesus, and yet our supreme desire is that our wills may be united with His will. As we meditate, we set Him before our eyes and look upon some part of His earthly life. We welcome His living Presence to our hearts that He may transform us from within. We offer Him our hands that He may henceforth act throughout our transformed lives.

In the days of this week we might meditate in this spirit upon such aspects of the life of Christ as: the Incarnation, the calling of the disciples, the Transfiguration, the Garden, the Trial, Calvary, Easter. Such a week of devout meditation should enable each one of us to live forever afterward more truly in the spirit of the words: "Christ before my eyes, Christ in my heart, Christ in my hands."

FOURTH WEEK: DEVELOPING A PATTERN FOR SPIRITUAL PROGRESS

Let us look back for a moment on our progress through the first three weeks. There has come an opening of our souls to God, a penetrating and growing knowledge of ourselves, and a more intimate awareness of the incarnate and living Christ. The brighter the illumination of God's Presence with us, the darker become the shadows cast by our unworthiness. We have begun to perceive our own inadequate and imperfect life. Our unwilling surface mind has been led to see its own sins. We have felt the winsomeness of Christ's faith in us, and the greatness of His love that will never let us go. But the bitter knowledge of our shortcomings and unworthiness, and the awakening sense of our response to God's high calling are only a half-way house on the road toward purification. Under the spur of our deepening love for God and our desire to turn from self-will to His will we now strive to develop a positive pattern for spiritual progress.

First Day: Humility. Pride is one of the universal enemies of spiritual growth. Yet how we all are beset in the most subtle ways by some form of pride and self-love! How shall we ever see God if we are looking only at ourselves? Consider the Master's parable of the Pharisee and the publican (Luke 18:9-14). Then, in the spirit of the week through which we have just passed, let us seek to have the ever-present Christ impart His humility to our inner souls. Graciously He invites us, saying:

"Come unto me, . . . for I am meek and lowly in heart." (Matt. 11:28-29.)

One of the Fathers of the Desert once compared the love of praise to an onion. When stripped of one skin it is found to be sheathed in another, and as often as you strip it, you will find it still protected. The same might be said of self-love. It is not enough to put it to death once by a definite act of self-surrender; it must be put to death daily. Beneath each sheath of self-regard and vainglory there is another; and if we think that the soul can be stripped of it once for all, we have still to learn the very elements of the spiritual life.[12]

We must then go forth into daily life striving to discipline ourselves to accept humiliations through the unpleasant tasks of our lives, through our daily inconveniences, through slights and reproofs, and all things that "go against the grain."

Second Day: Self-denial. We meditate upon the call of Christ: "If any man will come after me, let him deny himself, and take up his cross, and follow me." (Matt. 16:24.) If we are really to follow Him, there are crosses that we must bear. Bernard of Clairvaux says: "It is shameful that we appear as delicate members, shrinking at the least smart of pain, under a Head that is crowned with thorns." We must learn self-control; we must train our wills; we must discipline our actions. We must subordinate many of our pleasures to the will of God, and we must renounce dangerous pleasures. We must control our desires and restrain our imaginations. Our objective is not to cramp or mutilate our nature, but rather to free it from all that keeps it from God.

Third Day: Detachment. "For what is a man profited, if he shall gain the whole world, and lose his own soul? or what shall a man give in exchange for his soul?" (Matt. 16:26.) We are asked only to detach ourselves from anything that would hinder us from communion with God. We are asked to let go of the vain and foolish thoughts that occupy so much of our waking

[12] Herman, *Creative Prayer*, p. 119. Used by permission of Harper & Bros.

hours, for they dissipate the grace of God in our souls. We are asked to give up our inordinate love of things and possessions. We are asked to deliver ourselves from bondage to the opinions of men and to the delusions of flattery. We are asked to escape from vanity. And what is all this but the giving up of the lesser for the higher, of the shadow for the substances?

> All which I took from thee I did but take,
>   Not for thy harms,
> But just that thou mightest seek it in my arms.
>   All of which thy child's mistake
> Fancies as lost, I have stored for thee at home:
>   Rise, clasp my hand, and come! [13]

Fourth Day: Inner Discipline. We have often repeated the words of the General Confession: "Almighty God, Father of our Lord Jesus Christ, Maker of all things, Judge of all men; we acknowledge and bewail our manifold sins and wickedness, which we from time to time most grievously have committed, by thought, word, and deed, against Thy Divine Majesty." That confession is most sincere which leads most directly to a program for preventing the repetition of the failings which we have confessed. If we are constantly alerted, we can achieve an inner discipline which will strengthen us against surprise attacks. Our Master commands us, as He did his disciples, to "watch and pray, that ye enter not into temptation." (Matt. 26:41.) Using the letters of the word "watch" as the initials for five successive words, we can have a simple device to use as a check list for our daily lives. The five areas we are thus to watch are: words, actions, thoughts, companions, habits.

Now in our meditation let us seek to bring each of these into harmony with the spirit of Christ. Do our words reveal the accent of Christ? An early convert to Christianity was instructed to memorize a verse of scripture and then to practice it. When he had mastered this discipline, he was to come to the missionary for a new verse. Days and weeks passed, and he kept report-

[13] Francis Thompson, "The Hound of Heaven."

ing that he was still trying to practice the first verse which he had chosen. Finally he was asked what his verse was, and he replied: "I will take heed to my ways, that I sin not with my tongue."

Next let us check up on our actions. Have we done one thing today which only a Christian would? Or, on the other hand, have we been caught off guard and betrayed into un-Christlike attitudes, tempers, or deeds?

Now let us consider our thoughts. To what do our thoughts turn like a compass needle when they are freed from the duties of life? We are not responsible for chance thoughts that enter our consciousness, but we are culpable if we welcome them and cherish them. Martin Luther once said: "I am not responsible for the birds that fly over my head, but I am responsible if I let them build nests in my hair."

Next, what is our relation to our companions? Do we really love people? Are we kind to them? Do we realize that every person, no matter how unattractive, is a child of God? Is Christ through us helping people, or is the crowd influencing us?

Finally, we must consider our habits. Are they becoming patterns of effective living, or are they chains of imperfections? Few things are more revealing concerning the condition of our soul than an honest survey of our habit patterns.

As an aid to the discipline of our lives to the mind and spirit of Christ, let us frequently recall our Master's words, "Watch and pray, that ye enter not into temptation." Then let us honestly and sincerely pray and check our lives by this arresting word "watch"!

Fifth Day: In His Steps. "Christ also suffered for us, leaving us an example, that ye should follow his steps." (I Pet. 2:21.) As we have cleared away the hindrances to God's will in our lives, we have drawn closer to Christ. Now day by day let us seek humbly and reverently to follow Him. Like the minister in Charles M. Sheldon's book *In His Steps* let us continually front every situation asking, "What would Jesus do?" That we may be sensitized to His Spirit, let us consider the qualities in

Him which we want to have come alive in us. Are we patient with ourselves and with others? "No good ever comes of an impatient thought, word, or act, only and always a general lowering of the spiritual temperature." [14] Impatience throws us off balance so that we act in the wrong ways and say the wrong things. Do we take our faults and failures quietly? Have we learned not to seek position or power? Are we steadied within and unhurried in our lives? Have we spiritual staying power, perseverance and courage? Have we learned to master irritability, resentment, and anger? Are we in command of our fears? Now we seek to walk constantly in communion with the living Christ and from Him to receive grace to practice His virtues.

Sixth Day: Consecration. For years we have been bargaining with God. We have not been willing entirely to let go. We have made a pretense of our devotion, but we have reserved to ourselves many areas of our lives. We have resisted God's entrance into our heart of hearts. It is as if we are rather trying to pay rent to God than to let Him hold actual possession of our lives. "Self-surrender is not an isolated act, but involves a habitual and progressive discipline, a lifelong 'conversion' from love of self to love of God." [15]

As the love of God becomes more central in our hearts, self-surrender deepens into self-consecration. As we die to self-love, we awaken to love of God and love of people. We begin to have the mind of Christ in us, and we long to share in realizing His purposes. Our lives become charged with the creative activity of God. Our wills are becoming one with God's will, and therefore they are being tempered to steel. We grow courageous in our devotion to Him and His Kingdom. As our Master in the Garden prayed, "O my Father, . . . thy will be done" (Matt. 26:42), our deepest prayer becomes, "Thy will be done through me."

[14] Bede Frost, *The Art of Mental Prayer* (Milwaukee: Morehouse Publishing Co., 1931), p. 191.

[15] Herman, *Creative Prayer*, p. viii.

Seventh Day: Recollection. Throughout the spiritual exercises of the entire four weeks our object has been to become recollected, or God-centered. We have been trying to purify our souls and practice the Christian virtues in order that we might increasingly practice the Presence of God. We have sought to remove everything that hindered our oneness with Him. Now with deepened heart-communion with Him we walk in a growing sense of His nearness, a personal knowledge that "the Lord is nigh unto all them that call upon him, to all that call upon him in truth." (Ps. 145:18.)

Let us meditate upon a new spiritual program whereby our lives can be each day more continually centered on God. Let us consider how when we awaken in the morning we can adore, praise, and love Him; how we can then offer to Him all our thoughts, words, and actions for the coming day; how throughout the day we can frequently raise our hearts and minds to Him in ejaculations, or through acts of reverence, thanksgiving, and consecration; and how we can maintain our regular periods of devotion as the most joyous experiences of our entire day. Thus may we be led step by step to a deeper consciousness of His unseen but real Presence always and everywhere with us.

PART FOUR

The Way of Illumination

CHAPTER XIII

The Art of Communion with God

THE PRAYER OF SIMPLICITY—FIRST STAGE OF CONTEMPLATION

And ye shall seek me, and find me, when ye shall search for me with all your heart.   —Jer. 29:13

MOST OF US, AT LEAST A FEW TIMES IN OUR LIVES, IN SOME HOUR of personal crisis or in some supreme moment of spiritual exaltation, have been aware in a profoundly certain way that we were not alone; God was by our side.

This is what we mean by contemplation, which is the very heart of prayer. This deeper level of praying is well known to multitudes of simple and sincere souls who know nothing of the elaborately developed forms that others have found helpful in prayer. Every one of us has known such people—perhaps in our family or in our church—men and women who have directly walked with God. In our day thousands of youth have come back from places of extreme danger to tell us that, when they cried out into the dark after God, in an awesome and personal way He was by their side.

1. CONTEMPLATIVE PRAYER

Instinctively we know that this is a different kind of prayer from that which we and others have so often offered in a formal way. Here we sense that we are upon the threshold of a thrilling adventure that can lead us into a firsthand encounter with the all-powerful, sovereign, holy, loving Presence of God. Surely nothing in life can be as vital as such a possible

173

experience. To see how we can enter into the practical art of contemplative prayer is our present objective.

When we pass over its threshold, we are aware of a strange new realm within us, radiant with powers which we have hitherto glimpsed only in certain rare high moments. This realm is henceforth to be the home of a more vital form of praying and of living. It is an experience which should be normal for everyone who desires to grow and advance in his spiritual life. It is not an abnormal form of prayer. Really, what we have to fear in religion is not the fever heat and high blood pressure of some abnormal experience, but rather the anemic, low-pulsed, devitalized existence which arises from too much sub-normal Christian living. We desire a full-blooded, strongly constituted normality which is the true life of every vital Christian.

To make clear the more profound level on which the prayer of contemplation moves, let us recall the experience—such as many of us have had—of three or four hundred youth at a summer institute. Throughout the week religion had been more central in their thinking than during their lives as ordinary, average Christians back home. In morning and evening worship services, in group devotions, and in their high hours in chapel they had worshiped more frequently and more vitally than ever before. God was becoming more central in their thinking. It was more natural for them to center their lives on the reality of His Presence. In courses and discussion groups they had meditated upon the meaning of their faith and the relevance of the way of Christ to their world and their lives. Spiritual realities began to gleam before their awakened minds as something which impinged upon their own lives and demanded answers in terms of real action.

After a week of normal living together in Christian fellowship, and after the quickening of their deeper selves through the multiplying experiences of Christian worship, they came to the climax of the institute as they gathered about a campfire on one of the last nights. From the very beginning of this service there was a curious intensity and sense of realness in everything that was done. During the singing of hymns the words begin to come alive in their experience. When one of their leaders meditated upon the words of Christ to Peter, "Launch out into the deep," there was some stirring of consciousness as if they dimly sensed that across the ages the Master was calling still in the silent places of their hearts, calling for them to let go of the shore lines, to cease drifting in the shallows, and, in very fact, to launch out into the deep.

Then, suddenly and unaccountably, the whole experience deepened. It took on a new and different quality. The Spirit of God seemed to be really there. A profound quiet gripped each heart. God was talking to them, calling some to be ministers and some to launch out into the deep as his missionaries. The Spirit of God was challenging some youths to deal with hidden plague spots in their lives. It was all real and alive.

These youth had not drifted into this experience as a matter of mere emotion. It had come to them only after the spiritual retreat of a week of intensified Christian living and worship. How truly contemplative it was depended upon the preparation and response of each individual. It is even so for us in our individual lives of prayer. The price of contemplation is the development of our latent spiritual powers, and the disciplining of our nature for the pilgrimage to His Presence.

What is involved in this experience of contemplation? It is a living process which cannot be as neatly diagnosed and logically catalogued as can meditation, which is a more controlled experience. Meditation is a series of discernible steps; contemplation is a slope up which we mount to God's Presence. Here the free spirit is reaching Godward and, in turn, is being acted upon by the Divine. We can, however, discern the stages in the onflowing and developing spiritual process which tend to recur with some degree of regularity.

The transition between meditation and contemplation is affective prayer, sometimes called the Prayer of the Heart. This, as we have seen, is a form of meditation in which feelings surge up out of the deeps of us in response to Him whom we have glimpsed through the growing spiritual convictions at which we have arrived in mental prayer. It is a more personal and intimate outpouring of our hearts to God in love, praise, gratitude, reverence, contrition, and consecration. From this it is but a step to the simple, loving worship with which the contemplative experience begins.

2. SIMPLE CONTEMPLATION

Have you ever been praying, perhaps in a free, conversational way, when for some unaccountable reason the whole experience began to deepen? Your faith in God became so real that you found yourself pouring out your very heart to Him. It was as if His greatness overwhelmed you with awe, His holiness stirred you to deep reverence, His love was so personal that you poured out your answering love for Him. You were aware of the flooding into your soul of exalted and ennobling emotions to which your life heretofore had been almost a stranger. Then the tide of emotion slowly ebbed, leaving your attention curiously alive. Your whole being seemed centered on God. You no longer merely thought about Him. You were rather looking up to Him in a very simple, direct, and intimate way. His greatness and His love so filled your consciousness that nothing else mattered. All the external interests of life dropped away, and the eternal became vivid at the very center of your attention. Your whole personality was united in a creative focus upon the Presence of God—an experience which seemed hardly an act of your will, so completely did your love and interest center on Him. The prayers which you uttered were brief phrases that seemed to summarize the essential heart of your worship. You were intently reaching Godward in a most intimate spiritual conversation as with God in His very Presence. There were pauses of stillness which seemed not to interrupt but rather to intensify the lifting of your whole heart toward Him. The whole experience may not have taken a very long time, or it may have lasted for five or ten minutes. It may have come to you, briefly, on various occasions over a period of time in the midst of your other forms of praying.

The classic name for this experience, the Prayer of Simplicity, indicates the simplification or focusing of our prayer as compared with the more complex and ordered forms of mental prayer that precede it. In meditation we undertake to discipline our inward powers by deliberately considering and dwelling upon some aspect of reality—an attribute of God, a verse of scripture, an incident in the life of Christ. In the Prayer of Simplicity we frequently begin by returning to the process of meditation. We move on to a more glowing response to the Reality of which we have begun to be aware as we prayed. Then we find our prayer simplified. We are concentrating our attention upon one idea. We are dwelling upon it more than thinking about it. The mind enters into the deeps of itself and draws to a sharp focus of attention. God is very near, and in love we are apprehending to some extent His veritable Presence. We become recollected, or gathered together. We have really turned from self-centeredness to God-centeredness. The scattered interests of the self have been collected and brought to a creative focus. By a steady effort of the will, motivated by the deep love for God which has already been enkindled in the heart, the self concentrates its attention upon some aspect of God which is a part of our living faith. All discordant images are deliberately expelled from consciousness. With all of its faculties wide awake, the entire personality turns toward God.

This process is a very normal one. That is not to say that it is an average one, for all too few people put forth the requisite effort to attain the heights of their potential power of concentration. But whenever in any realm a person does put forth the highest effort of which he is capable, he can reach to a degree of willed attention which is one of the supremely valuable achievements of the human spirit. All too often our attention is scattered. A buzz of disconnected thoughts swarms through our minds; a kaleidoscope of evanescent pictures tumbles before our imaginations; gusts of variable emotion eddy up out of our instinctive impulses. Until we discipline ourselves and learn to control our attention, we are immersed in such a disorganized stream of consciousness. Real concentration lifts life to a new level in every realm. Supremely is this so in the realm of the spirit.

Learning to concentrate is not an easy accomplishment. The battle with distractions follows us as the inevitable heritage of the disorganized psychological pattern which characterizes such an overwhelming proportion of the rest of our lives. The mind we use in prayer is the mind that we bring to prayer. As we learn to control it in life, so also can we direct our attention toward God in prayer; and conversely, as we learn control in the place of prayer, we shall soon find its beneficent influence permeating the rest of our lives.

In our scientific age we are conditioned to interpret reality by analysis. We are content to describe it in terms of symbols— a mathematical formula, a working hypothesis, or a scientific classification and name. We are not accustomed to look search-ingly at reality in itself. Let us take a yellow rose in our hand and look at it—not examine it scientifically as a botanical speci-men of a particular genus and species, or analyze it in order to catalogue its parts, but rather look at it in itself. We are con-scious of it as a living thing, bearing within itself seeds of life which are the heritage of the roses of the ages and the prophecy of roses for a thousand years to come. Now we no longer think about it. We gaze at it. As we give ourselves utterly to viewing it, we are strikingly impressed. We so seldom give all of our at-tention to looking at anything that, now when we do, we see it with new intensity. We look at it contemplatively. We see its color as the light gleams translucently through it, the delicacy of its petals, the softness of its texture. It is immersed in an on-flowing stream of life. It has come out of the Universe; it was dreamed by the mind of God; it is an expression of the Life Principle which beats through all created things and survives in its fragile invincibility. Its beauty was shaped by the hand of the Divine Artist. Thus, in a moment of vivid apprehension, we see the rose in a way that makes its beauty and meaning ours forever.

Gazing at a rose in such a manner illustrates the heightened use of our normal powers which the contemplative experience involves. But when we come to prayer, in which we gaze devotedly upon God, there is a profound difference. In the first instance, we get from the experience what we bring to it. In the second, we get from God the wonderful gifts which He imparts. We can step upward from the contemplation of the rose to contemplation of God as its Creator. Suddenly it can become for us, not a picture of physical beauty, but a window into eternal Reality. We rise from appreciation of physical beauty to an experience of thankfulness and love for Him whose hand has given it, together with all life and all beauty, to us.

There are various pathways by which we rise to the Prayer of Simplicity. The one essential is that our whole devotional life shall have been enriched and matured, deepened and disciplined. What is required is both an increasing Christlikeness of character and a growing spiritual life of prayer. It does not matter by what route we have advanced. We can rise to this richer experience directly from a more worshipful use of the ritual materials of vocal prayer, or from profound meditation upon spiritual truths, or from spontaneous colloquies of our conversational prayer. This is a form of prayer which is the normal way of praying for practically all Christians who have advanced to reality in their prayer life.

It fulfills the very essence of prayer, which includes belief in God as a supreme Personality, assurance of the Presence of God near us and with us as we pray, and real communion between our hearts and our God. At this stage of contemplative prayer, however, we have not yet reached the place where the Divine Presence manifests itself with that immediacy and overwhelming objectivity which comes at the climax of contemplation.

3. THE SIMPLE PRAYER OF COMMUNION

In analysis we may distinguish affective prayer, which is a form of meditation, from the experience of simple communion with God in the first stage of contemplation; but in practice they merge into one another. We may see this if we study the prayer of Martin Luther. He begins with devotional discipline in meditation, but only as preparation for the outpouring of his heart in affective prayer that becomes simplified into direct outreach toward God. He says:

I am sometimes so cold and cheerless that I cannot pray; then I close my ears and say, "I know God is not far from me, therefore I must cry to Him and invoke Him." I say, "O Lord, hallowed be Thy name, Thy Kingdom come, etc." Thus my prayer grows warm and fervent. An excellent help and expedient for awakening prayer is to read, sing, and hear God's Word, and read through the Psalms carefully or even attend the ordinary service of the church. And the heart gradually becomes warm and the Spirit is kindled in us.[1]

In Luther's background was the fact that he had "passed through the school of medieval mysticism, and had taken up into his devotional life its most precious qualities, its grand individualism, its heartfelt intimacy with God, and its gentle love of Christ." He was therefore "able to enrich with a mystical element the simple and vigorous devotional religion of the Bible without dimming or distorting its purity."[1] A childlike simplicity speaks in Luther's prayers. He poured out the deep necessities of his heart and conscience in free conversation which ended in quiet surrender and joyful trust.

Luther's prayer at Worms is a typical example of the ebb and flow of moods and feelings in passionate, spontaneous prayer. It begins with a woeful consideration of himself in his grievous situation. His fate is uncertain; no reliance is to be placed upon man: "The bell has been already cast, judgment has been pronounced." The anxious thoughts mount up (into) a cry of com-

[1] Heiler, *Prayer*, p. 131. Used by permission.

plaint: "Ah God, ah God, O Thou my God." Passionate entreaty for help is wrung from the soul of the tormented man: "Stand Thou by me; do this, Thou must do it, Thou alone!" His trust increases with the thought of the worth and justice of his cause: "The matter is not mine, it is Thine." Growing confidence is again stifled by rising doubts, which burst forth in vehement questioning of God: "O God, dost Thou not hear? My God, art Thou dead?" The petitioner threatens God with losing faith in Him, but his indomitable trust banishes doubt: "No, Thou canst not die; Thou only hidest Thyself." He prays afresh, "Stand by me." Once again uncertainty and fear gain the upper hand: "Lord, where tarriest Thou? Where art Thou, O my God?" Finally, all doubts are scattered; the strain is relaxed; faith triumphs over uncertainty; hope is victorious over fear. Heroic determination fills him who but lately hesitated and trembled, who complained and questioned: "Come, come! I am ready, even to forsake my life for this, submissive as a lamb, for righteous is this cause which is Thine." He faces death boldly, for whether living or dead, he feels himself under the protection of the Most High; nothing evil can come to him. "And should my body perish for this cause, should it fall to the ground, yea, be broken to fragments, yet Thy word and Thy spirit are enough. And all this can happen only to the body; the soul is Thine and belongs to Thee and will remain forever with Thee." [2]

The spontaneity and reality of this prophetic prayer of communion with God is far more than a superficial colloquy or a meditation. It involves the experience of the Prayer of Simplicity, the ardent yearning outreach of the soul in true communion with God. To pray, for Luther, is "to come into God's Presence and to speak with Him." On another occasion he expresses his amazement "that I who am only dust and ashes and full of sins should speak to the true, living, eternal God."

This recognition of prayer as simple communion with God is likewise true of the other great leaders of the Protestant Reformation. To pray, for Calvin, is "a conversation with God"; for Zwingli, "to go to God," "to be acquainted with Him and speak with Him." Bunyan says, "By prayer is our most direct and immediate personal approach to the Presence of God." This living communion with God is under the impulsion of the Holy Spirit. We might well describe the Prayer of Simplicity in Jude's phrase "praying in the Holy Spirit." Luther writes, "When the Holy Spirit specially touches and stirs the heart then prayer is wont to become very hot." George Fox says, "We pray publicly and privately as the Holy Spirit inspires us." John Bunyan states, "It is impossible for the heart to pour itself out without the Spirit's help."

This form of simple communion with God expresses itself sometimes in importunate yearning, sometimes in spiritual petitions, sometimes in brief, energetic, and passionate ejaculations, sometimes in conversation with the Divine Friend who is right by their side as they pray. We have already noted Luther's cry: "Ah God, ah God, O Thou my God." We hear John Bunyan cry out: "O Lord, I beseech Thee, show me that Thou hast loved me with everlasting love." Then from this outreach with its consciousness of complete dependence upon the higher will of God comes a vital feeling of the nearness of God. When contact is established, there is direct touch with God. This experience is described in these words of Söderblom, "In the depth of our inner life we have not a mere echo of our own voice, or our own being, resounding from the dark depth of personality, but a reality higher and greater than our own, which we can adore and in which we can trust."

4. SIMPLIFICATION OF LIFE

The Prayer of Simplicity is accompanied by a growing simplification of our lives. Achieving simplicity in life is not some far-off, otherworldly device of medieval mysticism; it is the most practical and desperate need of our modern age. Life has grown so complex, its demands upon our time are so pressing, and its allurements so overstimulating that we have grown tired and nerve-racked. Deeper than that, we are involved in soul-shattering inner conflicts between our deep self with its unquenchable ideals and our accommodations to our environment. Our urgent drives toward meaning, purpose, and security in life are thwarted and blocked by the secularism, escapism, and defeatism of our times.

No more penetrating analysis of the real disease of the soul of modern man has been given than in the last chapter of Thomas R. Kelly's *A Testament of Devotion*. It points out that we tend to place the blame for our conflicts on our environment, when all the time the real solution is an inner lack of simplification, or integration, of our own lives.

Strained by the very mad pace of our daily outer burdens, we are further strained by an inward uneasiness, because we have hints that there is a way of life vastly richer . . . than all this hurried existence, a life of unhurried serenity and peace and power. If only we could slip over in that Center! . . . Life is meant to be lived from a Center, a divine Center. Each one of us can live such a life of amazing power and peace and serenity, of integration and confidence and simplified multiplicity, on one condition—that is, *if we really want to. . . .*

Let me talk very intimately and very earnestly with you about Him who is dearer than life. Do you really want to live your lives, every moment of your lives, in His Presence? Do you long for Him, crave Him? Do you love His Presence? . . . Have you set yourselves to be His, and *only* His, walking every moment in holy obedience? . . . "Thou shalt love the Lord Thy God with all thy heart and soul and mind and strength." Do we really do it? Is love steadfastly directed toward God, in our minds, all day long? Do we intersperse our work with gentle prayers and praises to Him? Do we live in the steady peace of God, a peace down at the very depths of our souls, where all strain is gone? . . .

Do you *want* to live in such an amazing divine Presence that life is transformed and transfigured and transmuted into peace and power and glory and miracle? If you do, then you can.

There is a way of life so hid with Christ in God that in the midst of the day's business one is inwardly lifting brief prayers, short ejaculations of praise, subdued whispers of adoration and of tender love to the Beyond that is within. . . . One can have a very busy day, outwardly speaking, and yet be steadily in the holy Presence. . . . I am talking about a revolutionary way of living. Religion isn't something to be added to our other duties, and thus make our lives yet more complex. The life with God is the center of life, and all else is remodeled and integrated by it.[3]

5. HOW WE PRAY IN SIMPLICITY

To make practical suggestions for such an intimate and sacred form of prayer is exceedingly difficult. There are really no rules. In the higher ways of devotion we are increasingly led by the Spirit. But in the rich experiences of many people we may find a few suggestions to make as concrete as possible our understanding of the practice of the Prayer of Simplicity. As has been suggested, we may enter upon this pathway whenever any form of prayer in which we are engaged becomes truly God-centered, whenever we stop merely thinking about God and instead approach Him directly with sincerity and love. If the way lies through meditation, some form of the pouring out of our hearts in affective prayer is the usual transition to this higher form of communion with God. Then, in the intimacy of His Presence, we converse with Him freely and easily. We talk to Him in a simple, loving manner.

At this, or some other point in our simple prayer, there arise from our souls *acts of devotion*. These are of the same nature as those used in vocal prayer or as preludes to meditation except that they are briefer, more direct, more deeply felt. They rise spontaneously out of our hearts and become the vehicle of our communion with God. They are primarily acts of love, which is not merely emotion but an act of will. Love is far more rugged than a transient eddy of feeling. We now reach out directly in an act of love toward God. This is so central that the Prayer of Simplicity might well be called "the practice of loving prayer." Then there are acts of thanksgiving, of hope, of faith, of adoration; and there are, also, acts of earnest resolution which differ from the planned responses of meditation by

[3] New York: Harper & Bros., 1941, pp. 115, 116, 119, 120, 122, 120, 121. Used by permission.

being a very immediate reaction of our souls to the promptings of God's Holy Spirit. We are becoming attuned to His guidance, and our consciences are being sensitized to the mind of Christ.

Our prayer becomes still more intimate. There are pauses of meaningful stillness out of which frequently the soul, yearning toward God, breaks forth in vocal or inward ejaculations. These are the tidal responses of the soul to the upward drawing of the Infinite. These ejaculations again are far richer than the spontaneous little "javelin" prayers that we have sent speeding up toward God out of our daily lives. They are aspirations, the upward yearnings of our spirits. Shirley C. Hughson in his book *Contemplative Prayer* points out that we are not in prayer to use vain repetitions but that this does not mean that we are to avoid calling again and again upon God as did our Lord Himself in Gethsemane, "saying the same words." There are expressions from the Psalms, from the Gospels and the Epistles, from hymns, and from the words of devout Christians which can be repeated with a strong, loving will and intention in a way that will make every repetition bring a profounder realization of God's Presence and love. Then he adds:

But note well that this is not a truth which one can realize by merely being told of it, or by reading about it in books. We must experience it. Go into some quiet place, some place where perhaps you can speak aloud without disturbing others or being interrupted, and with heart, will and entire attention and intention set powerfully upon God, cry, "Father, Father, Father," not thinking anything about Him, but calling Him again and again as a trusting child might call in the dark to a loving father. After the first cry, pause; keep an intense silence within, and hearken. Then cry again, "Father, Father." Your experience will be unique if you do not find in some such simple devotion a very close drawing to the Father's heart. Other expressions, the repeating of the Sacred Name of Jesus, or a loving address to the Holy Ghost, may be found of equal help, and as our experience deepens we shall find profit in many expressions which will be readily suggested to us.[4]

[4] New York: The Macmillan Co., 1935, p. 179. Used by permission of Holy Cross Press.

Meaningful prayers of aspiration which come immediately to mind are: "O Love of God!", "Jesus, I love Thee," "Almighty God," "My God and my All," "Christ, we do all adore Thee," "Heavenly Father," and many others. These are repeated with ever more intense concentration of devotion. We call on God as we simply gaze on Him with love. It is for this reason that this Prayer of Simplicity has sometimes been called the Prayer of Simple Regard. Bernard Iddings Bell tells of a boy who went into a church to pray. The rector, observing that he had done this on several occasions, asked him what he said to the Lord in his prayer, and he answered with childlike simplicity, "Oh, I was just loving Him awhile." Perhaps it was with the thought in His mind of the spontaneity of such prayers that Jesus said, "Except ye be converted, and become as little children, ye shall not enter into the kingdom of heaven." (Matt. 18:3.)

It is possible to use ritual prayers as contemplative acts of devotion. We could thus use our Lord's Prayer, or the Sanctus, or the familiar Collect for Purity of Heart, or any others with which our converse with God might be enriched. In some way we lift our hearts to God, breathe forth our love, rejoice in His omnipotence, goodness, beauty, and love; and worship Him with the spontaneous outflow of intimate devotion.

Hughson ends his book with this spiritual call:

A few quiet minutes devoted today to the exercise of holding oneself calmly, lovingly, resolutely in the presence of God, will open the gates of the soul, that God, entering in, may fill it with the infinite strength and sweetness of His love which is His essential Self; and this will mark for us the beginning of a new and nobler way of life. It is a rich opportunity. Let us give ourselves to it generously, and see if God will not show us a fullness of joy, an access of spiritual power, beyond all that the past has wrought.[5]

[5] *Ibid.*, p. 186. Used by permission of Holy Cross Press.

CHAPTER XIV

Beside Still Waters

THE PRAYER OF QUIET—SECOND STAGE
OF CONTEMPLATION

He leadeth me beside the still waters.
—Ps. 23:2

IT IS DIFFICULT TO PRESENT NEAT DIAGRAMS OF THE SUPREME activity of the living soul when it rises to moments of communion and contact with God. Principal L. P. Jacks once said that the rational attempt to do this is like hunting a fox from a railroad train. The human spirit refuses to walk down any set roadbed bounded by straight steel rails. We are dealing here with a creative process which is always free and spontaneous. "The wind bloweth where it listeth." Increasingly is this so as we approach the high places of the human spirit. We find that our descriptions are at best diagrammatic. They do, however, help us to recognize the stages which recur with a certain degree of regularity, and they also carry helpful suggestions for our growth in the practice of His Presence. We have already discussed the beginnings of the process of contemplative prayer. We now come to the second stage of our upward progress toward the secret place of the Most High, the Prayer of Quiet.

As you have been praying, have you not sometime had the whole experience suddenly deepen into stillness? Your words faltered into silence, you became aware of a curious quiet far deeper than the initial stilling of the soul with which you had become familiar in the experience of worship. You passed over the threshold of quiet unwittingly and normally. You came to

187

a poised moment of expectant waiting. Your mind was vitally alert, but at the same time it was not actively exerting itself. You were so receptive that if you had used words they might have been: "Speak, Lord, for thy servant heareth." Once you have experienced this strange inner quiet you will know that of which we speak, for it is so distinctive that you cannot fail to recognize it.

This Prayer of Quiet is familiar to many of us as the Simple Prayer of Attentive Openness which is so much used by the Quakers. George Fox describes it in this way:

Be still and cool in thy own mind and spirit from thy own thoughts, and then thou wilt feel the principle of God, to turn thy mind to the Lord, from whom strength comes, whereby thou mayest receive His strength and power to allay all blusterings, storms and tempests. That is it which works up into patience, . . . into quietness, up to God with His power. . . . Therefore, be still awhile from thy own thoughts, searching, seeking, desires, and imaginations, and be staid in the principle of God in thee, that it may raise thy mind up to God; . . . and thou wilt find strength from Him, and find Him to be a God at hand, a present help in time of trouble and in need." [1]

1. SILENT CONTEMPLATION

The characteristic of this stage of contemplation is an intensely vivid silence. We see now that the stillness we cultivated in earlier stages of our pilgrimage is something far more vital than a surface technique. Our earlier training in the fine art of stillness has but prepared us for this more real experience of quiet waiting on God, which is the beginning of our deepest communion with Him. The process of introversion likewise reaches its summit in the curious deepening of consciousness which takes place in the interior stillness. We are coming to a knowledge of the ground of the soul where we feel most deeply our kinship with the Eternal, and the action of God's Holy

[1] Douglas V. Steere, *On Beginning from Within* (New York: Harper & Bros., 1943) , p. 83. Used by permission.

Spirit deep within us. We now more perfectly understand the beauty and profundity of those treasured words: "Be still, and know that I am God." (Ps. 46:10.)

The Prayer of Quiet continues the experience of the Prayer of Simplicity. Only here the aspirations are even briefer and more fully experienced. In the spontaneous Prayer of Simplicity we were crying out to God from the fullness of our hearts. Here all within us continues to cry out after the Infinite, but the cry rises from deeper levels. Simply and adoringly we contemplate the Infinite God. There may at first be brief acts of devotion and simple aspirations, but soon these pass into the silence of wordless prayer. We have come to the colloquy of silence, "a wordless blending of love in the immediate Presence of God." We are silently gazing on God and pouring out our affections, adoration, and praise directly rather than verbally. With willed, loving attention we are reaching toward God. "The substance of this work is naught else but a naked intent directed unto God for Himself. . . . Look that naught work in thy wit nor in thy will, but only God." [2] This experience of silent contemplation might be called a state rather than an act of prayer. It is because we have grown to love Him, to adore Him, to pause overwhelmed by reverence in the sense of His nearness that we are impelled to turn with such determined persistence toward the place of His Presence.

2. COMPLETE CONSECRATION

As the soul concentrates its attention upon God, it turns from its surface self to its deep self. Here we have withdrawn into the very citadel of our hearts. The assaulting sensations of the external world, the distracting imaginations of our picture-making faculties, the disturbing fluctuations of our emotions, the labored processes of our logical thinking, and the accusing voices of our hidden memories are all left behind as the spirit mounts upward to the fullness of its concentration on the Divine. The intellect needs to learn how to be still no less

[2] *The Cloud of Unknowing*, pp. 100, 132.

than the body, if it is to concentrate its powers on the work of hearing. This bringing of the mind away from its distractions and restlessness to a single and sustained attention to God is the crux of the whole matter.

This is very far from making the mind a blank. It is the filling of the mind with God to the exclusion of all else. We are not passive in the sense of inaction, for we are engaged in the supreme spiritual action of our lives. We are passive in the root meaning of the word, for we are suffering our lives to be acted upon by the "Supreme One." It requires powerful, persistent, strenuous, spiritual discipline to hold the soul thus at attention, waiting upon God.

Augustine Baker, in his *Holy Wisdom*, describes this state as an eagle soaring in the heights of heaven "with a great swiftness, but withal, great stillness, quietness, and ease, without any waving of wings at all, or the least force used in any member, being in as much ease and stillness as if she were reposing in her nest."

As we wait thus quietly in a dawning awareness of God's nearness, love utters its silent demands. As our hearts are warm with love for Him, we desire wholeheartedly that nothing shall interfere with our communion with Him. We sense dimly that the Spirit of God is working in the silent places of our souls, searching out the secret recesses of our being that there may be nothing in us which He does not wholly possess. We come to understand that the more complete our consecration, the more perfectly can God enter within us. Our desires are stretching out in love toward God. We make a complete consecration of our wills to Him. We want no neutralizing evil to enter or to live in us. We cannot bear to be separated from the God of such love and wonder. Our attention is deliberately detached from all that is not God. In profound humility we bow in unreserved submission to His sovereign will as we say:

> Breathe on me, Breath of God,
> Till I am wholly Thine,

> Till all this earthly part of me
> Glows with Thy fire divine.[3]

3. RECEPTIVITY

In the Prayer of Quiet our personalities have been brought into a profound inner harmony. Our consciences are now at peace. We are released from inner conflict. The powers of our souls have reached a supreme integration. Our disciplined God-ward pilgrimage has reached a high plateau. Now there comes an immense relief from strain. The soul, wholly filled with love, rests in God. Like a child of the Infinite, it rests in the Father's arms. The bliss of inward peace is now most fully ours.

While this emptying of the self and the achievement of passive waiting upon God is a characteristic element of the Prayer of Quiet, it is a preparation for something other than itself. It is a means to an end—the full experience of God's Presence in the Prayer of Active Contemplation. It is an essential precondition of God's deep self-communication to the soul. Shirley C. Hughson says:

When we hold ourselves in the presence of God, attentive and receptive, not trying to think them; not considering any images of the imagination, good as they may be in themselves; but actually hearkening, the ear of the soul attent, waiting with no element of impatience in our attitude—at such times it is that the channels of communication between God and the soul are wide open, and God Himself, as distinct from any mere intellectual knowledge or revelation concerning Himself, flows into us.[4]

In the words of an ancient hymn:

> Could but thy soul, O man, become a silent night,
> Christ would be born in thee, and set all things aright.[5]

In the Prayer of Quiet we have been slowly brooding upon the Eternal and paying loving attention to God. We have been

---

[3] Edwin Hatch.
[4] *Contemplative Prayer*, p. 147. Used by permission of Holy Cross Press.
[5] Quoted in Herman, *The Meaning and Value of Mysticism*.

surrendering our deep selves in attention to Him. We have come to an experience which is like a deeper conversion, a giving of our very self to Him in love. Then there has come a resultant peace, an inner harmony, an almost complete absence of tension and strain. In the Presence of God's greatness our pride has been lost in humility. We are now detached from the nonessential. It is a withdrawal such as all creative action necessarily involves. Meister Eckhart says of the man thus at prayer: "He keeps himself in silence, stillness and peace so that God may speak and work in him."

The Prayer of Quiet is usually of very brief duration. It is a transitional state introducing the praying soul to the Presence of God. In it man ceases to pay attention to the messages from without in order that his prepared soul may be attuned to hear the eternal messages that speak within.

God is very near, and in love we are apprehending to some extent His veritable Presence. We have become recollected, or gathered together. We have really turned from self-centeredness to God-centeredness. Quieted, steadied, waiting, expectant, our souls scarcely move in the moment of their most creative outreach after God. Dimly we begin to sense His nearness and, obscurely as in a Cloud of Unknowing, His Presence.

> When inmost cloud and darkness brood
> I kneel in depths of quietude
> O adoration holy!
> Better than best that earth hath heard
> Is uttered now without a word
> To loving heart and lowly.[6]

Some years ago in one of the great art galleries of Munich, the Alte Pinakothek, I walked with a party of tourists while the guide lectured volubly about various pictures. There was the commotion of many people discussing the masterpieces, looking up references in guidebooks, and questioning the lecturer. At

---

[6] Tersteegen, quoted in Heiler, *Prayer*, p. 178.

length I detached myself from the crowd and slipped back alone into one of the rooms. Before me was the picture of the Crucifixion by Rubens. I stood alone in silence gazing upon it; and now for the first time I began to see it—the rugged power of the composition, the appealing beauty of the color, the dramatic intensity of the portrayal. Then the room seemed to grow very still. (Or was it not rather that my heated heart grew quiet?) The picture quickened in me a realization of the scene which it portrayed. I seemed to be transported in thought back to Calvary itself and to be looking at the actual Crucifixion of the Christ. I could feel the weight of His body hanging down from the cross. I could see His face of suffering love—never to be forgotten. I began to think of the deeper meaning of that strange Man upon the cross against that dark and threatening sky. Then the quiet grew deeper still. I bowed my head in silent prayer. I was no longer gazing at a picture but looking through a window of eternity, not looking at His tortured form as on "a green hill far away" in the distant past, but aware now of the living Presence of my Saviour in the room with me as I prayed. It is only in the stillness of solitude, away from the crowd, that we truly apprehend a masterpiece; it is only in the awe-filled quiet of the deeps within that we perceive the Presence of the Divine.

CHAPTER XV

The Secret of His Presence

THE PRAYER OF ACTIVE CONTEMPLATION—THIRD STAGE OF CONTEMPLATION

He that dwelleth in the secret place of the most High shall abide under the shadow of the Almighty. —Ps. 91:1

HOW GREATLY OUR AGE NEEDS A FRESH DISCOVERY OF THE WAY into the Holy Presence of the Almighty! Perhaps as we now consider the experience in prayer known and practiced by those men and women who have through the ages truly lived their spiritual lives in awareness of the Most High, we may find some personal clues to help us on our pilgrimage to the secret place of His Presence. We are now concerned with making real the next stage in that art of "humble, steadfast, brooding attentiveness to the things of eternity in the solitude of our own souls" which will lead us to the heights of contemplation.

1. COMING INTO LIVING TOUCH WITH GOD

As we pass imperceptibly from the Prayer of Quiet to the Prayer of Active Contemplation, the stillness in our souls deepens profoundly. Into this deep pool of quietness within us comes the stirring of the inner waters. We are in the Presence of God. We know, with the directness and the immediacy by which we know contact with a friend through love, that we are in touch with God. There are overtones of objectivity which bring the deepest certitude that our lives have ever known. There is an inner radiance of joy and an illumination of our whole being. There is a peace, not of ourselves, that is breathed

194

into us as a divine gift. There is a sense of life being lifted, in complete normalness, up to the very summit of possible human experience. For a brief moment we have been with God, and then it is past; and yet in a sense it never passes, for once we have stood in His Presence life can never be the same again. We now know Him whom we have believed. Nothing can ever again shake us from the objective certitude of this experience. In profound actuality, through His mighty grace, we have been where God is, in the very reality of His holy, majestic, living Presence. This is the Prayer of Active Contemplation, and the fullness of the experience of illumination.

It is an experience which is in no sense abnormal, but one which leaves thrilling overtones of a heightened normalness of life, of a deeper steadiness and integration of the human spirit, of a more powerful desire to live abundantly in a world which is now radiant with the sense of the reality of God's Presence. This is an experience at which every devoted Christian can and should arrive. It is not reserved for a few mystic souls but is the privilege of all of us who have become deeply enough Christian to enter into the fullness of our spiritual birthright.

The Prayer of Active Contemplation is the experience resulting from the preceding stages. But it is more than they. In the first stage we have found ourselves looking directly at God in Himself; in the second stage we have found ourselves aware of His immanent nearness; now we enter the very immediateness of His Presence. Or rather, God Himself completes the highest process of His universe when in His greatness He graciously draws near to His created children revealing His divine Fatherhood, His incarnate Love, His real Presence. This is a brief experience. It is a glimpse, but a glimpse of the very heart of Reality. It is a touch, but the touch of the very hand of God upon us. It is the holy, awesome wonder of man at the top note of the human spirit receiving the visitation of the Most High.

Many of us find the reality of God's nearness in nature. By

this I do not mean merely a rapt gazing upon its beauty or a sensitive responsiveness to the awe and wonder of some mighty spectacle. This may precede it, but we must not confuse the two experiences. The psalmist said, "I will lift up mine eyes unto the hills," but he did not stop with an appreciation of their majestic heights. He asked, "From whence cometh my help?" Then he stepped from the mountaintops into the presence of the Infinite and made answer: "My help cometh from the Lord, which made heaven and earth." It is when we grow deeply quiet and wait with reverent openness of heart that sometimes we too pass from some wonder of His creation into the living Presence of the Divine Creator.

One time at sunset I sat alone on the rocky brink of the Grand Canyon of the Colorado. With a friend I had driven out near Desert View. For a while we had shared the grandeur of the scene, then had separated so each might find a vantage point to take in the beauty in solitude and in quietness. From where I was perched on the rim, the great walls dropped precipitously down to the Tonto platform and then to the dark granite gorge in which the Colorado shone silverly in its tortuous course far below. The colors which filled the mighty chasm were unbelievably beautiful—the deep red of the layers of sandstone, the alternating cream-colored strata of limestone, and the dark green accents of the trees were blended into subtle harmonies by veils of soft mist that flushed and deepened with the ever-changing light of the setting sun. One moment the whole scene palpitated with glowing amethyst; the next it deepened into thrilling rose light; then as the sun sank behind a cloud the haze turned into a living blue which was shot through in the distance with rays of gold. As twilight muted the almost unendurable glory, the depths beneath became an abyss of silence, so vast that the great winds seemed scarcely to breathe in them. The awesome majesty of towering buttes, sculptured by the ages, loomed up in shadowy masses out of the still depths.

Involuntarily I found myself praying: "O God, how great is Thy power! Thou hast laid these dark foundations of our world. Thou hast reared up these mighty mesas and these stupendous walls. O Thou Almighty One, fill my weakness with Thy power! O Thou who hast moved upon the face of these deeps creating these wonders through immeasurable aeons of time, hush the tumult of my heart in the sweep of Thine eternity! O Infinite Spirit of Illimitable Beauty, lift my soul above the dust and tawdriness of life! O Presence Divine, whose peace broods over these ageless heights and fills the abyss with stillness, make my spirit quiet within me." As reverent wonder overwhelmed me, my prayer deepened into a quiet awareness of His immanent nearness and passed into the awesome moment when I knew He was there in all the mighty power of His Presence. The afterglow of twilight trembled into the dark, lighted by eternal stars. ("Through the stillness Thou hadst spoken, O my God!") After a long time I left the edge of the canyon where the great depths were lost in the mystery of night. I rejoined my companion bearing an incommunicable thing in the silence of my heart.

The experience of illumination comes, however, not only in crisis hours, nor amid the wonders of nature, but most often to the prepared heart of him who has risen to the Prayer of Active Contemplation. A classic description of this high moment comes to us from the *Confessions* of Augustine:

My mind withdrew its thoughts from experience, extracting itself from the contradictory throng of sensuous images, that it might find out what that Light was wherein it was bathed. . . . And thus, with the flash of one hurried glance, it attained to the vision of THAT WHICH IS. And then at last, I saw Thy invisible things understood by means of the things that are made, but I could not sustain my gaze; my weakness was dashed back, and I was relegated to my ordinary experience, bearing with me only a loving memory, and, as it were, the fragrance of those desirable meats on the which as yet I was not able to feed.[1]

[1] Book VII, ch. xvii.

Augustine is a profound theologian, and his native genius is metaphysical; yet these high moments of vision and flashes of spiritual insight, when he came into living touch with God, have been called the most influential moments of his life.

Here at the heart of contemplation in this experience of illumination man at last achieves his supreme destiny: he comes into living touch with his God. The meeting is so real, so immediate, so natural, so profoundly steadying, and so convincingly objective that man knows he has been in the veritable Presence of God. Again and again, as our souls are disciplined for this high perception, we shall find in the midst of a conversational prayer, or at the climax of the outpouring of our heart in affective prayer, or while engaged in corporate worship, or while gazing upon the works of God in nature, this simple intensification of life about God, this centering of our attention on Him, and then this breathless pause, this strange deep stillness, this expectancy upon the threshold of the eternal, and then the supreme moment, brief but illimitable, when His Presence reveals itself in living contact with the deeps of our soul.

Sometimes the very simplest Christians, who may nevertheless be the most sincere, find that they have advanced unwittingly to the level of contemplation as their normal experience. Their background of faith attained through years of devotional reading of the Bible, their purgation achieved through years of disciplined Christian living since their conversion, have made God so real in their daily lives that they have but to close their eyes for a little while in the reverent worship of prayer to be ushered into the august Presence of the Almighty. Thousands of the devout members of all churches enter daily the realm of *contemplative prayer*. They are at home with God in perfect naturalness. Deep calleth unto deep in the quiet sincerity of the communion of their hearts with the Heavenly Father. It does not matter by what road we have traveled; the important thing is that we have risen to the plane of humble, sincere, spiritual intimacy with our God.

It may be that such visitations of the Eternal will not come frequently to many of us in prayer. They are always the gifts of His grace and come to us only through the action within us of His Spirit. Our task is to love Him greatly, to serve Him devotedly, and to draw near to His Presence constantly. Sometimes we grow spiritually more than we realize in times of aridity. But as we pray, the high moments of illumination will come; and, touched by their light, our life of prayer will be forever more radiant, and our walk with God more intimate.

Those who have been in the very Presence of God come back unable to tell the world in words just what they have experienced, but they do bring an unshakable certitude that they have been with God. So far as they can explain it, they speak of a deep stillness, deeper far than the conscious stilling of our souls in vocal or mental prayer. They tell of a concentration of personality where all else but the Presence ceases to exist. They tell of a receptivity in which willed action ceases, as always when we completely open life to any mighty reality. They refer to contemplation in which meditative thought is silenced, and they gaze with awe upon the Eternal. They sometimes are aware of words, or insights, that have arisen, stimulated by God, into their inner consciousness—impressions that bear indubitable overtones of a Divine Voice. They recall a Presence so objective as never again to be doubted. It comes through a normal experience, but with life so heightened by its inner synthesis and its objective visitation from on High as to touch the peak of possible human experience.

2. ILLUMINED INSIGHT

In illumination there has been revealed a new power of perceiving Reality more validly, more vividly, and more vitally than ever before. It is one of the capacities that lie dormant in all of us until they mature through the discipline of life. It is allied to the flashes of insight which come to artists, musicians, prophets, philosophers, and scientists in their moments of supreme creativeness. Mozart described how an entire symphony would rush in a torrent of creative energy into his mind. The themes, the counterpoint, the instrumentation would flame into reality. He said, "I can comprehend it in my mind at a glance (as one does a beautiful picture or a beatutiful person), and not bit after bit as it is heard later on in imagination, but simultaneously. What has thus come about I do not easily forget, and perhaps this is the best gift God has given me." This power of creative insight might be called synoptic vision, the power to see things together as a whole by one comprehensive glance of the mind.

This power to perceive is undeveloped in most of us, but it is brought into play in the Prayer of Active Contemplation. It is a new way of seeing Reality. It is not counter to reason. It builds upon it and goes beyond it. It is not merely feeling with a limited and subjective validity, though it is motivated by the most exalted and ennobling emotions that sway the human spirit. It is not merely a will to believe that which we wish to believe. Rather it is strongly willed attention to that which on other grounds has been approved as the deepest conviction of our rational faith. It is not imagination in the sense of a projection of something that is within us; for we have disciplined ourselves to turn from our ego, from our self-centeredness, from our self-consciousness, from our self-will, to the highest extent of which man is capable, and to gaze only on that which we know on the most convincing grounds to be real. Rather it is the summit of our powers integrated, fused, poised in the total response of our whole personality to Reality. It includes and transcends feeling, conation, and reason. It is their harmonious fulfillment in togetherness of expression. It is their fusion into unity of action as in all profound, or complete, apprehensions of beauty, truth, love, or goodness. The indivisible personality is functioning from the center of its highest integration.

If this insight is called an intuition, it must be distinguished sharply from a subnormal intuition, or a hunch. This latter is merely a vague projection of the subconscious and is always of very doubtful validity. Illumined insight, on the other hand, is intuitive in the sense that it is a power of knowledge obtained, without recourse to inferential reasoning, by a synoptic grasp of Reality. It is based upon the totality of our past reasoning, faith, and experience. It is a flash of comprehension having the nature of the ultimate way whereby, in any realm, man most vitally and creatively grasps truth. These insights may afterward be tested and criticized by reason, and they should be. However, the data of religious experience come not from rational analysis; they are given in spiritual perception. It is through this high but normal power of illumined insight that man, at the summit of his experience in prayer, comes into direct awareness of the Presence of Almighty God.

3. OUR AWARENESS OF GOD'S PRESENCE

Poulain points out that this spiritual knowledge of God is the result of an impression of a special kind. This spiritual impression is not to be equated with an imaginative impression. This could not be the way to enter into real correspondence with pure Spirit. It is a spiritual impression by which God makes known His Presence; it is something interior which penetrates the soul. It is substantial; that is, it partakes of the very substance of Reality. God is near us and in us.

God Himself is active in this process. We must never forget that it is the Heavenly Father who is approaching us and drawing us to Himself. It is the action of the Holy Spirit working in the deeps of our responding souls that is the ultimate ground of the reality of this experience. It is the Presence of the Living Christ, who is with us always, that stands at the door and knocks; and, as we discipline our souls to hear His voice and open the door, it is He who enters. If there is any reality to religion at all, there is an ontological basis for our awareness of the Presence of God.

Teresa exhibits an unusual power of analyzing her innermost experiences and a very sane balance of evaluation and discrimination. She points out that what is experienced within is first a consciousness of the Presence of God, "certain inflowings of the Godhead," a consciousness of the Divine Immanence. Then, again, she distinguishes over against this a sense of Presence that is concrete and definite—the invisible Presence of the Living Christ. Concerning one of her own experience she writes:

I was in prayer one day . . . when I saw Christ close by me, or, to speak more correctly, felt Him; for I saw nothing with the eyes of the body, nothing with the eyes of the soul. He seemed to me to be close beside me; and I saw, too, as I believe, that it was He who was speaking to me. . . . As the vision was not imaginary, I saw no form.

When later she was questioned, "How did you know that it was Christ?" she replied, "I do not know how I knew it; but I could not help knowing that He was close beside me." Very humanly she adds, "There are no words whereby to explain—at least, none for us women who know so little; learned men can explain it better." Then she continues:

For if I say that I see Him neither with the eyes of the body nor those of the soul—because it was not an imaginary vision—how is it that I can understand and maintain that He stands beside me, and *be more certain than if I saw Him?* If it be supposed that it is as if a person were blind, or in the dark, and therefore unable to see another who is close to him, the comparison is not exact. There is a certain likelihood about it, however, but not much, because the other senses tell him who is blind of that presence: he hears the other speak or move, or he touches him; but in these visions there is nothing like this. The darkness is not felt; only He renders Himself present to the soul by a certain knowledge of Himself which is more clear than the sun. I do not mean that we now see either a sun or any other brightness, only that there is a light not seen, which illuminates the understanding, so that the soul may have the fruition of so great a good. This vision brings with it great blessings.[2]

4. THE INNER VOICE

These inner perceptions can be influential and powerful. We test their validity by their life-enhancing quality. We discover that those experiences are most true which leave us physically, mentally, and spiritually better. They infuse new strength, spiritual knowledge, and a compelling sense of direction. It is for this reason that through the ages all that have risen to the heights of contemplation have said that this experience of the Divine Presence is "from God."

Similarly, they have experienced interior convictions, definite calls, irresistible commands which have been as the speaking of an Inner Voice in their souls. Here quite often words rise, God-stimulated, into their consciousness. There are none of what one of the great contemplatives, the author of *The Cloud of Unknowing,* calls "the monkey tricks of the mind." There is a definiteness and concreteness to these words that are formed within us. They are not corporeal; no audible voice speaks them; our ears do not hear them; they are inspoken. All of us have experienced a similar reality in the voice of conscience within us. Surely most of us have also received assurances of divine encouragement and intimations of the divine will when we have prayed.

Sometimes our consciousness of God speaking in the depths of our souls may come as a call to duty, a challenge for consecration, or guidance concerning some vital decision. E. Stanley Jones graphically records such an experience:

One day, as a young man, I placed a letter on a chair and knelt before it. The answer to that letter would determine my lifework. The Inner Voice said, "It's India." I arose and said, "Then it's India." That clear moment was a real moment, and has held me

[2] *The Interior Castle,* ch. xxvii, 2-5.

steady amid low moments of discouragement about the details of India.[3]

There is need for caution in this matter of the Inner Voice. When we ask, "Do we get guidance in prayer?" the answer comes almost unanimously from those who know most about the inner experience, "Yes." But we do not receive it on a superficial plane. To be attuned and ready to receive God's guidance means that we have disciplined our lives to His will. Real guidance is costly—sometimes as costly as Gethsemane. When we seek God's will, He may reveal it to us in a cup which we must drink or a cross which we must bear. Jesus received divine guidance, but only after that awesome prayer in the Garden. We should not expect that we can be silent for a brief time, write down any vagrant message which comes into our mind, and say, "This is divine guidance." We do receive real guidance, but it comes with validity only after we have paid the price of the disciplines of devotion and the adjustment of our lives to God's will. No less an authority than John of the Cross, one of the greatest of the contemplatives, says:

I am really terrified by what passes among us in these days. Anyone who has barely begun to meditate, if he becomes conscious of words of this kind during his self-recollection, pronounces them forthwith to be the work of God; and, convinced that they are so, goes about proclaiming "God has told me this," or "I have had that answer from God." But all is illusion and fancy; such an one has only been speaking to himself. Besides, the desire for these words, and the attention they give to them, end by persuading men that all the observations which they address to them are the responses of God.[4]

There do come touches of God's guidance, but they are far above the level of hunches or vague subconscious prompt-

[3] *Abundant Living* (New York and Nashville: Abingdon-Cokesbury Press, 1942) , p. 254.

[4] Underhill, *Mysticism,* p. 275. Used by permission.

ings. Those that arise from real contact with the Divine always carry overtones of objectivity. They force themselves upon our attention, often in spite of our resistance. As we follow their leading, they are always verified by their results. True guidance from the Inner Voice represents the action of God's Holy Spirit in the moments of our highest psychological integration, profoundest sense of responsibility, truest moral insight, and most selfless consecration to the will of God. They are checked against the highest spiritual standards to which the soul has been sensitized in prayer: surrender of self-will to God's will, clarity of our perception of the mind of Christ, and conviction of personal duty and social responsibility. Upon this high level the guidance of God's Spirit does come increasingly in the still deeps of God-centered contemplation.

Sometimes the Inner Voice brings to us divine assurance and encouragement as we front one of the crowded hours of life. On one occasion there came to me a sudden emergency which necessitated an immediate operation. The surgeon left me alone in a small consulting room while he telephoned to complete arrangements with a near-by hospital. The brother of one of my staff members, a man of my own age, had died with the same condition just ten days before. The shock of the unexpected discovery clouded my soul. In the brief time when I was left alone, I prayed. For a little while all remained dark; then suddenly out of the inner stillness there arose the words, "I am with you." They bore such irresistible overtones of objectivity that I knew that they were not merely something that had arisen out of my own subconsciousness. They were so powerful as to be life-changing. They made an immediate difference. The whole situation and my outlook upon it was instantly changed. All fear and anxiety vanished. An infinite peace steadied my spirit and restored my poise. With the words there had come a profound sense of His Presence. In a very real way He went with me through the experience. His peace during all those hours was the most wonderful I had ever experienced.

205

5. RADIANT LIVES

Our experience in the Prayer of Active Contemplation lights up our entire life. As our own personalities are flooded with inner radiance, they seem to impart a glowing splendor to the world—or is it that they perceive the splendor of God that always dwells there? Of this experience it has been said: "Poems of intolerable loveliness will bud for us on every weed." The world is charged with the grandeur of God. As Meister Eckhart said: "We see God everywhere." We have been in a very real sense initiated into the spiritual universe.

God's Spirit works in our souls transformingly. Our temporal lives have been indwelt by the Eternal, and they can never be quite the same again. We have given ourselves utterly in prayer; we have met with our God. For one supreme moment we have felt the touch of God upon our minds, our affections, and our wills. Now we are moved to offer our entire personality to Him in a supreme oblation. Henceforth all of life is to be a sacrament of practicing the Presence of God.

CHAPTER XVI

Listening to the Agony of God

THE PRAYER OF VICARIOUSNESS—FOURTH STAGE
OF CONTEMPLATION

I am crucified with Christ: nevertheless I live; yet not I, but
Christ liveth in me. —Gal. 2:20

KAGAWA OF JAPAN IS ONE OF THE UNIQUELY CREATIVE CHRISTIAN
characters of our age. He transcends national boundaries and
stands out as one of the great world Christians of our day.
Strange power seems resident in him. It is a power that has
been harnessed to tremendous movements of social uplift. The
burden of the slums was on his heart; he threw his very life
into their transformation, and they were transformed. The
ruthless exploitation of human personality—especially the
lives of little children, under the intolerable conditions of the
advent of Japan's machine age—stabbed his conscience; and
he pioneered until there came nationwide reform. He shoul-
dered the burdens of the farmer. He organized a co-operative
movement that has had world-wide influence. When Japan
struck against China, he went to China to ask as a Christian
for forgiveness. He was arrested by the army and thrown into
prison. The vision of Christ dwelt in his heart, giving him
steadfastness and joy. He said, "I felt the peace from above."
He was condemned to death. But then the minister of foreign
affairs intervened, and he was released. In the midst of war he
still witnessed for the way of Christ. Spiritually he is the most
potent evangelistic force in his nation. The leaven of his life
is helping to bring redemptive hope to his people.

What is the secret source of such effective living? One memorable afternoon I asked him this question, and very soon our conversation turned to prayer.

"How," I queried, "do you pray?"

He thought at first that I was interested in the outer form of his prayer habits.

"I do not pray a long time before retiring at night," he replied. "I just pray briefly and commit my life to God, and then go to sleep at peace and trusting in His care. Then," he continued, "I awaken about two o'clock in the morning and pray for a brief time until three. I retire again and sleep until morning. Then I awaken and begin the day with prayer and live through the day conscious of His Presence."

There flashed into my mind immediately the words of one of his poems:

Day ends:
Breasting the North,
My shoulders shiver
As I onward go.
And yet,
I utterly forget
The cruel cold,
Nor feel the dark,
Because my heart
Aches with the people's woe.

Oh, let me trust
That through my tears
God's Kingdom has
One little inch drawn near!
Then what is it to me
That my weak body be
Beaten to dust?
Midnight:
I crawl from out my bed
Into the cold,

And gaze up at the stars again,
Finding God there
To help me bear
My daily load
Of grief and care,
Sorrow and pain.

Deep in the night
Our spirits meet,
And prayer is sweet! [1]

Here is a man, busy with multitudinous social projects and thronged with the cumbering burdens of mankind, for whom prayer is so central that he takes the very quietest hour of the night for deep communion with the Eternal. Prayer is so much a part of his life that he really prays without ceasing, but this special hour holds a fascinating place at the center of his experience. Even while traveling in America, he told me, he had not missed this vital hour five times on the entire trip.

But I was interested to discover, if possible, the very heart of his inner power. Our conversation, lasting for a considerable time, was wrestling with the deeper things of the spirit. We seemed to be trembling on the verge of a disclosure that might have profound value if I could only grasp it. I was impelled to press into the very inmost sanctuary of this remarkable man's soul. Spiritual reticence held him back.

"That is a secret story," he said at length. "When I get to heaven and see the angels, I will tell the words I have heard." But then he added, "Once in a while in a little group where they ask me I tell of it."

"For this deeper prayer," I then asked, "how do you begin? What is the first step?"

"Surrender," he replied instantly.

I knew that he was not using the word in a negative or purely passive way, for he is patently the opposite of a passive

---

[1] *Songs from the Slums* (Nashville: Abingdon-Cokesbury Press, 1935), pp. 72-73.

soul. And so I asked further, "But just what do you mean by surrender?"

"A letting go of self into God," he answered. I can still see his hands as he gestured to express that complete letting go of self at the center, and the turning of the human heart utterly toward God. In that moment I caught a glimpse of one of the deep primary acts of powerful prayer.

But I pressed still further into those intimate depths of his experience: "How do you accomplish this deep surrender of yourself to God?"

"It is praying like Jesus," he said. "He went into the Garden of Gethsemane and so let go of Himself that He became fully conscious of God. He reached up, entering into His very heart. He felt the love of the Eternal Father suffering over the aching wounds of the world. *Jesus listened to the agony of God, and then He incarnated it.*"

Awhile he was silent. I waited to see what would be his final word. He was still brooding upon the praying Christ in Gethsemane. Then in deepest sincerity he said, *"In prayer I listen to the agony of God, and then I surrender myself to Jesus."*

I knew now that I had touched the very inner soul of Kagawa's life. As I looked at this small, vibrant man, his life again flashed before me—how he had become aware of the aching wounds of his own people, how he had burdened himself with the whole situation, how as a young Princeton graduate just returned to his own country he had lived in the filth and squalor of the slums that he might share their awful degradation and somehow lift their blight from his people. I recalled how he had endured beatings and hunger for their sakes. He had fathered them and fought for them and led them. He had held the neglected babies in his arms. He had stood by the side of little children whose lives were being slowly crushed out in factories. He had tried to bear the burdens of his people, and dreamed of a co-operative Christian order which would lift crushing loads from many lives. He had felt the tragic evils of the military, and tried to save his country from a savage fate.

And always he was trying to evangelize his country, to make Christ real as their Saviour. This little man whose strength had been impaired, whose eyesight had been dimmed, whose body had been battered and wounded by the burdens that he bore, had in this fleeting moment of insight revealed the dynamic of his life.

What if prayer could become that for each one of us—a profound communion with the Christ-hearted God whose love agonizes ceaselessly over His suffering world! Not one of His children shudders beneath a burden or bows beneath a tragedy but that the wound goes to the very heart of God! If we truly commune with the Father whose heart was laid bare on Calvary, we shall never again be able to evade a sense of spiritual responsibility for helping His wounded children.

1. VICARIOUS CONTEMPLATION

But how can we pray like this? It is immediately apparent that we cannot rise to these supreme heights of prayer without much discipline of our spiritual life. The entire pilgrimage of prayer must prepare us for this transcendent experience. It can begin very simply in the earlier discipline of vocal and mental prayer. But at its highest this vicarious sharing of the passion of Christ is intercession lifted to the contemplative level. We may call it the Prayer of Vicariousness and consider it the fourth stage of contemplation.

When we discuss the classifications of contemplative experience, we must always bear in mind that they are only analytical diagrams of an organic, living experience. Almost every qualified writer varies in his interpretation or emphasis. Teresa, for example, changes her classifications to some extent in each of her principal works. This variation but reveals that we are here dealing with a spontaneous level of prayer where our spirits are freely communing with the living God.

The first three levels which have been described are usually made explicit under one name or another in writings on contemplative prayer. The fourth level is also almost always referred to in some way and is implicit in almost every analysis. A moment of reflection reveals how inescapably this is so. When we experience the illumining moment when we are consciously in the immediate Presence of God, what is He like? He is in very fact Christ-hearted. Contact with the Christ of God is the very center of our deepest awareness of the Divine. How can we be aware of the loving redemptive Heart of God in living reality and not be quickened to some vicarious response?

This experience is distinctive enough to be singled out and emphasized as an essential stage of contemplation, not only because we thus commune with the Living Christ, but also because it is, in itself, *sui generis*. What happens within us then is a vital and new aspect of contemplation. It is our interaction with the Divine as distinguished from our communion and contact with His Presence. The Prayer of Simplicity is our supreme experience of communion with God. The Prayer of Active Contemplation is our high point of contact with His living Presence. The Prayer of Quiet is the transition which partakes of the nature of both these experiences. The Prayer of Vicariousness is the lifting of our spirits to a new level of interaction with the redemptive love that beats in the Heart of God. While all four stages contain some degree of communion, contact, and interaction with God, yet each characteristically emphasizes the one which has been designated.

We further see that all four of the major dynamic movements of the soul toward God find fulfillment in one of the stages of contemplation: recollection in Simplicity, stillness in Quiet, awareness in Active Contemplation, and response in Vicariousness. There are elements in the Prayer of Vicariousness which indicate that it is a transition between contemplation and the higher life of oneness with God in the Transforming Union. In its essence, however, it is a form of ordinary prayer to which all Christians are summoned to advance.

2. APPREHENDING THE CROSS

As we enter upon the pathway that leads up to the experience of the Prayer of Vicariousness, the first necessity is that we should recapture a vital awareness of the Cross. There should be for all Protestants more Cross-centered prayer. We so often become vitally aware of the Cross only on Good Friday. What if, in remembrance of that sacred Friday which all the Christian world so hallows, we might make every Friday the day of the week on which to meditate on the Cross. We do not frequently enough turn our steps to Calvary. Teresa once said: "For the many that come to Bethlehem, there be few that will go on to Calvary."

The story of Christ's passion should be read with brooding insight. We should seek the stimulus of choice devotional books on this subject. Then at certain times—perhaps on seven consecutive days—we should center our attention upon the last words that He uttered. What unplumbed depth of meaning we might discover in each phrase! A symbol of the Cross can constantly recall our thoughts to His passion. We should meditate long upon the great prophetic chapter, Isaiah 53, which, whatever its original setting may have been, was appropriated by Jesus as the spiritual picture of His life. Its words should get into our memories and into our hearts. There are hymns which pulse with the meaning of the Cross. Whatever our rule and practice of prayer may be, there is need for a deeper apprehension of the Cross. Let us set apart some sacred prayer period on every Friday to center our gaze on Calvary and thus keep it as a Day of the Cross.

It would be a deepening experience for every one of us to lay out a course of meditation that would enable us to pray our way into the great mysteries of Christ's life. Teresa said concerning her meditations:

This was my method of prayer; as I could not make reflections with my understanding, I contrived to picture Christ within me; and I used to find myself the better for thinking of those mysteries of His life during which He was most lonely. . . . I did many simple things of this kind; and in particular I used to find myself most at home in the prayer of the Garden, whither I went in His company. I wished, if it had been possible, to wipe away that painful sweat from His face. . . . I believe my soul gained very much in this way, because I began to practise prayer without knowing what it was.[2]

To picture vividly and appreciate vitally the experiences of the Upper Room, the Garden, the Trial, and the Cross surely would draw us nearer to an understanding of His passion. No practice can be more helpful here than the Sulpician Method, which was presented in our discussion of meditation. You will recall its emphasis upon a consideration of our Lord's life under two aspects, as historical acts and as eternal states. Calvary is an act taking place there and then, but how much more is it a permanent state! We think of Jesus in His earthly life, and then we adore Him in His eternal reality. In prayer we seek to put on the mind of Christ and to become one with His desires and His will. We contemplate Christ on the cross in order that we may incarnate His love in our lives. We are advised not to allow a two-hour interval to pass without raising ourselves to Jesus our Saviour in some act of love or adoration. John Eudes (1601-80) says, "The Christian life is nothing else but a continuation and achievement of the life of Jesus in each of us; . . . *so should we be as Jesus on earth.*" Our prayer first becomes adoration, in which we consider and look upon Jesus Christ in love and reverence; then communion, in which we unite our hearts with the spirit of Him whom we love and adore; and finally co-operation, in which we unite our wills with His will and resolve to reproduce the life of Jesus in our own actions. This intimate spiritual method of prayer certainly would lift our devotion to a high level. We might come to understand the prayer of Teresa when she said:

Christ has no body now on earth but yours,
No hands but yours,

[2] *Life,* IX. 4; cf. IV. 10.

No feet but yours.
Yours are the eyes through which is to look out Christ's compassion
  to the world;
Yours are the feet with which He is to go about doing good;
And yours are the hands with which He is to bless us now.

Our apprehension of the Cross, however, moves beyond the
mental prayer of meditation and this more affective form of it
to the higher levels of Contemplative Prayer. Angela of Foligno
describes how, as she contemplated "that sharp sorrow which
was in the soul of Christ . . . , *I was transformed into the
sorrow of the Crucified.*" [3]

At Alverna Francis of Assisi prayed: "O Lord, my Saviour,
I ask two favors before I die: let me feel in my soul, in my
body even, all the bitter pains which Thou hast felt. And in
my heart let me feel that immeasurable love which made Thee,
Son of God, endure such sufferings for us, poor sinners." [4]

Many Christians find in the sacrament of Holy Communion
an occasion for the Prayer of Vicariousness. While our concern in this book is with the prayer life of the individual, we
must always remember the stimulus and richness which is
brought to individual worship by participation in corporate
worship. The Sacrament may be participated in merely on
the level of vocal prayer or mental prayer; but it may also be
apprehended on the level of a contemplative experience. In
simplicity we gaze with awe and adoration upon the Christ of
God and His sacrifice for us. In profound stillness and receptivity we open our hearts to Him in the Prayer of Quiet. To
many souls there then comes a moment of active contemplation
as they sense the spiritual Presence of the Living Christ.

> How through this Sacrament of simple things
> The great God burns His way,
> I know not—— He is there.

[3] *Visions and Instructions of Blessed Angela of Foligno*, ch. 31.
[4] *The Little Flowers of St. Francis* (Everyman's Library; New York: E. P.
Dutton & Co., 1947), pp. 113-14.

The silent air
Is pulsing with the presence of His grace,
Almost I feel a face
Bend o'er me as I kneel.[5]

The communion, contact, and interaction with Christ which takes place in our hearts during the Sacrament reaches its climax in the Prayer of Vicariousness.

Of this Evelyn Underhill writes:

Only this act of love can wake the creature's love, and call forth the self-offering of that creature to the Transcendent; in self-oblation, consecration, and sacrifice. This truth is the very heart of the Christian mystery. It is fully declared on Calvary, and again set forth in every Eucharist.

The true intercessor offers the oblation of his imperfect love, that it may become a channel of the Absolute Love. Here he prays from the Cross.

Understood in the deepest sense personal worship is man's return-movement of charity to the inciting Charity of God; . . . first in surrender to His pure Being, and secondly in loving co-operation with His creative activity.[6]

3. THE SUMMIT OF INTERCESSION

In discussing intercessory prayer we noted how we were, through an achieved state of spiritual communion with God, co-operating with the divine purpose. There is a profound truth in the statement that "the Spirit itself maketh intercession for us." (Rom. 8:26.) The God who indwells our hearts is active in us when we pray. As in the Prayer of Vicariousness we rise into conscious oneness with His Spirit, we gradually perceive that we are, in the prayer itself, performing one of the greatest actions of the human spirit.

It is not only the Holy Spirit which "maketh intercession for us." We remember how Jesus made intercessions for individuals and for mankind while He was here on earth. But if

[5] G. A. Studdert-Kennedy, from "At the Eucharist." Used by permission of Harper & Bros.

[6] *Worship* (New York: Harper & Brothers, 1937), pp. 341, 167.

this is so, then when Jesus as the Son of God prayed, God talked with God. We are here upon the threshold of the ultimate mystery of the Godhead. Surely neither the Holy Spirit nor Christ needed to recall things that had been forgotten by the Father. Rather is it that in the awesome communion of such divine intercession we glimpse the vital heart of the very essence of the Unity of the Trinity. Eternally the yearning love of God lives and acts within His nature. In these divine intercessions there is revealed the everlasting, redemptive activity of God, which was incarnate in Christ, and which is today mediated by the Holy Spirit. This is the supreme work of the Godhead for man's salvation.

It is part of the eternal activity of the ascended Christ—"He ever liveth to make intercession for them." (Heb. 7:25.) Such an intercession must not be thought of as a petition. It is the offering of oneself in the fullness of the powerful action of eternally continuing love. Perhaps this is the mysterious reason for the statement that the intercessions of the Spirit are made "with groanings which cannot be uttered." W. E. Orchard makes the penetrating observation:

This extraordinary description, only expressible in human language by means of paradox, gives us some notion of the enormous labour that intercession involves, and of the force it is necessary to employ, in order to bring human souls nearer to God, the Spirit striving, as it were, to bring our reluctant humanity into that orbit of energy by which the impulse of the divine love constitutes Father, Son, and Spirit one indivisible Unity. This gives us some idea what a power intercession can and must exert, as well as shows more clearly how perfect intercession can only be exerted by one who is so one with God that he can make others one with Him too.[7]

Such prayer is so far beyond the ordinary conception of intercession as to deserve to be called the Prayer of Vicariousness. Here we glimpse that our action for the Kingdom of God

[7] *Prayer*, p. 84. Used by permission of Harper & Bros.

means not alone what we do with the practical concerns of earth, vitally important as they are, but also what we do in spiritual action with God in the heights of prayer. When we pray in such a spirit, we must be willing to be wholly, utterly, and at any cost, expendable "for their sakes" to bring about God's Kingdom on earth. But we must also attain to such closeness of union both with God and with man as shall make us one with the spiritual power of His eternally creative action.

4. APOSTLES OF THE LOVE OF GOD

If we thus really come near to the mind and heart of God, we shall develop what the Quakers so beautifully call a "concern" for mankind and what the earnest evangelicals of the past referred to as "a burden for souls." In prayer we shall enter into such a close union with Christ that the things He lived and died for—the taking away of the sins of the world, the making of peace, the bringing of souls to God—are constantly in our minds. We shall become apostles of the love of God which dwelt in Christ Jesus our Lord.

Prayer at its highest then means a deep personal sharing of the passion of Christ. Whenever we deeply pray and enter into living communion with God, we become vividly aware that we are in touch with a Christ-hearted God. This profoundly colors all truly Christian prayer. It is the root of the primary distinction between Eastern mysticism and Christian mysticism. The former ends in quietism, withdrawal from life, passivity, negative self-loss in nirvana. On the other hand, Christian mystics are the great actives. While they realize that prayer is their highest action, they nevertheless come forth from this transfiguring experience impelled to act with all their powers for God's Kingdom in the world. There is a healthy-mindedness and a life-giving quality to all truly Christian mysticism. This is a vital distinction which many commentators have overlooked.

The dynamic of the apprehension of the Cross in prayer is now, and has been through all centuries, the central power of the Christian movement. The keynote for all Christians is expressed in Paul's statement: "I am crucified with Christ: nevertheless I live: yet not I, but Christ liveth in me." (Gal. 2:20.) The early Christians felt that God was in Christ reconciling the world unto Himself. They personally experienced the Presence of the Living Christ; they shared His Spirit; they carried on His work; they believed that Christians must incarnate the reality which they discovered in Christ, knowing that it is central in the eternal life of God. Whenever we return to this personal awareness of the Living Christ and share His concern for the life about us, we link up with the most powerful tradition of the Christian Church through all the ages.

In prayer, thus, "we listen to the agony of God," and then "we surrender ourselves to Jesus." We become one with His great love. For us the Cross is not past but present. The passion of Christ did not end on Calvary but is continuous. Christ is the Lamb slain from the foundation of the world. Today where human anguish is greatest, Christ is nearest. He is alive, and in living Presence walks among the sufferers on the battlefield, kneels beside the wounded, lingers among the patients in hospitals, roams by the side of the starving and dispossessed multitudes of the earth, pauses in infinite pity in all lands where little children fall to "wither like rosebuds on a dusty highway." Where tortured minorities tremble with terror, there the strong, silent Christ must go. In every place where Christ bends over human suffering, you and I, His followers, belong. Prayer is lingering in His presence until His spirit surges through our lives, calling us to Christlike adventures in service and compassionate ministries of mercy.

As we contemplate the Man of Sorrows and become one with His suffering love, we begin to participate in His feelings for mankind. We are sensitized to the cry of need all about us. There is an old legend in India concerning a saint. One bitterly cold night his followers found him shivering from the cold.

They hastened to their homes and brought blankets with which to cover the saint, but his shivering continued. Then one of his disciples, with more insight than the rest, took his blankets and went about the village until he found a neglected little child shivering with the cold. He covered him and warmed him. When he returned, the saint had ceased to shiver. It is sensitivity of this degree that develops in a Christian who has lingered in prayer near the heart of Christ. "Inasmuch as ye have done it unto one of the least of these my brethren, ye have done it unto me." (Matt. 25:40.)

This is the spirit of a missionary like Melville Cox crying out as he gave his life for Africa, "Though a thousand fall, yet let not Africa be given up." It is the spirit of John Knox as he prays, "Lord, give me Scotland, or I die." It is John Wesley's concern for England in his day. It is the inner power of a love like that of Schweitzer as he ministers in Christ's stead to the people of the Congo today. When we have really prayed the Prayer of Vicariousness, we come down from this high experience, as from a Mount of Transfiguration, endowed with a divine power for the healing of the open wounds of the world.

One Sunday I shared with my congregation Kagawa's deep experience of the Prayer of Vicariousness, recalling his haunting words, "Jesus listened to the agony of God, and then He incarnated it," and his deep personal revelation, "In prayer I listen to the agony of God, and then I surrender myself to Jesus." Included among the worshipers that day was a long-time friend, Georgia Harkness. A little later, inspired by these words, she wrote the following poem:

> I listen to the agony of God—
> I who am fed,
> Who never yet went hungry for a day.
> I see the dead—
> The children starved for lack of bread—
> I see, and try to pray.

220

I listen to the agony of God—
  I who am warm,
  Who never yet have lacked a sheltering home.
  In dull alarm
  The dispossessed of hut and farm
  Aimless and "transient" roam.

I listen to the agony of God—
  I who am strong,
  With health, and love, and laughter in my soul.
  I see a throng
  Of stunted children reared in wrong,
  And wish to make them whole.

I listen to the agony of God—
  But know full well
  That not until I share their bitter cry—
  Earth's pain and hell—
  Can God within my spirit dwell
  To bring His kingdom nigh.[8]

[8] *The Glory of God* (New York and Nashville: Abingdon-Cokesbury Press, 1943), p. 16.

PART FIVE

The Way of Oneness with God

CHAPTER XVII

The Heights of the Spirit

MYSTICISM

If any man will come after me, let him deny himself, and take up his cross, and follow me. —Matt. 16:24

PRAYER IS THE GODWARD REACH OF A MAN'S SOUL. IT EXISTS ON many levels and has many degrees of intensity and power. Prayer is communion with God, contact with God, the feeling of the Presence of God, our intimate oneness with God. It can be a primitive and elemental cry in an hour of danger, the expression of a felt need; it can rise to the level of worship in a more God-centered prayer; or it can rise through the various degrees of contemplation where man stands in the veritable Presence of God until at last he reaches the height where the Spirit of God acts in a vital and transforming way within his soul. Accompanying the developing prayer experience is a process of life-adjustment to the will of God. In the higher experiences of prayer these two actions of the one soul are seen to coalesce. God is at work within the soul transforming and enhancing the personality and lifting it into living awareness of the reality of the Divine Personality.

The highest experiences of life and prayer with which we shall be concerned in this chapter and the next are mystical experiences. The stages of prayer which we have discussed up to this point are not fully mystical although there have been mystical elements in the last three stages of contemplative prayer. It is well for us to be clear as to just what is meant by the term "mysticism" before we proceed.

1. CRITERIA OF CHRISTIAN MYSTICISM

a. It Is Not Neurotic or Pathological. True mysticism and profound prayer always lead to normalness and healthy-mindedness. No one can deny that there have been mystics who have suffered illness and have had at least borderline conditions of abnormality. Such pathological symptoms or states are, however, no part of true mysticism. This much can be said with assurance: Any pathological condition is separate from and counter to the classic constructive Christian stream of high religious experience. Insofar as it has any connection with mystical experience, it is a dangerous bypath that should be resolutely avoided.

Someone may object, however: "What you say is true. Certainly all religious experience should be wholesome. But are not the states of ecstasy and rapture by their very nature abnormal?" It should first be pointed out that there is much testimony from the mystics themselves in support of the position that ecstatic experiences are not essential to the highest experience of God. We cannot, however, entirely rule them out as rare possibilities in the lives of religious geniuses. We recognize them as an element in the experience of some of the Old Testament prophets whose lives and religion attain to the highest moral plane and to the loftiest spiritual levels. Paul and John apparently entered into the full meaning of ecstasy. There are other Christian experiences of such an intense nature as to come under this classification.

But the essential results of such ecstatic experiences are always wholesome and constructive. They represent a love of God that is kindled into flame, a devotion that has become heroic, a quest for God which unites the whole being in an intensity of adoration. This concentration upon God is so complete that the consciousness of the external world is not merely blurred as in contemplation, but is almost entirely excluded. Paul speaks of being "caught up to the third heaven" (II Cor. 12:2). The Holy Spirit is at work within the human soul, producing a more profound awareness of God, which is the preparation for creative action.

It has been pointed out that unless the effect of ecstasy is "a great holiness of life even to the point of heroism," the experience itself is open to suspicion. Francis de Sales says:

A soul may be transported beyond herself in prayer; but if she be not habitually united to God, and elevated to the divinity by a life superior to nature and the senses; if her conduct does not visibly display that ecstasy of action and operation which is accomplished by a renunciation of worldly desires, of self-will, of the inclinations of corrupt nature, and the practice of interior virtues, as humility of heart, meekness, simplicity, a constant tender charity for our neighbor, raptures serve only to attract the admiration of men without rendering her more pleasing to God.[1]

Not merely is there this moral and Christian test of the effects of ecstasy in life and action, but also there must be a psychological test of its normality. Abnormal, pathological states resemble true ecstasy only in a very external way. Hallucinations, for example, are visual, oral, or tactile representations of the imagination. Such phenomena are largely discounted by mystics, who place the emphasis instead upon an intellectual, or synoptic, perception of eternal meanings in God that are in no way sensory. The abnormal patient is weak in will, divided in personality, depressed and dull. His moral sense is frequently atrophied. Christian mystics on the other hand have, as Poulain has pointed out, three diametrically opposite characteristics:

1. They are strong characters, the originators of projects that are vast and difficult of execution. They are guided not by imagination but by reason. 2. Their will is so strong that they fight against all opposition in order to bring their enterprises to a successful termination; but they fight, above all, against themselves; and the prolonged labour, which they have had to overcome in order to

[1] *Love of God*, Bk. VII, ch. vii.

practise certain virtues, fills us with astonishment. We, who think that we have iron nerves, do not feel ourselves capable of such a succession of efforts. 3. They all have a very high moral ideal with which they are constantly occupied: the desire to forget self in order to devote themselves to the glory of God, and to the temporal or spiritual good of their neighbour. The saint is not a degenerate but a hero.[2]

A Christian mystic remembers his vision, and retains it in consistency with his classic faith and his critical reason. This is rare in psychopathic experiences. The mystic can bear pain. In fact, he not merely accepts it; he triumphs over it. This is by no means true of the neurotic or the depressed.

To sum it all up: Ecstasy is not an essential of the highest attainment of the life of devotion. Most of us who now desire to climb the very highest pathways to the Presence of God will not experience it. When it does come, it is by action of the Holy Spirit of God alone, and is totally beyond our power to attain in ourselves. All ecstasy must meet the criteria of psychological normalness, of Christian meaningfulness, and of life enhancement in terms of effectiveness in action. And what we have said about ecstasy applies also to all of the higher states of the soul. They are never abnormal psychologically, and their results are always wholesome. They never disintegrate the personality. They always produce a stronger integration of life. They are therefore not to be feared by anyone.

b. It Is Not Pantheistic. The highest experience of prayer and devotion is called the Transforming Union with God. Most of us immediately react against that word "union," conceiving it to be some form of pantheism. There have been historic mystics who have so regarded this experience, but the distinguishing mark of true Christian mysticism is the total rejection of the pantheistic conception. We are not here concerned with a self-loss in nirvana. The central emphasis in the teaching of Christ is the sacred value of the individual in God's sight. The autonomy and integrity of the human personality

[2] *The Graces of Interior Prayer,* pp. 259-60.

is guaranteed by the very nature of God through His love and redemptive grace. The identity and continuity of the human personality, as a sacred bearer of eternal values, is treasured and preserved by Almighty God; it is never transgressed.

To understand the nature of union with God we must not conceive of it upon the plane of a physicochemical concept of union, in which one quantity is taken into and becomes part of another quantity. The concept which explains it best is derived from personal experience and is of the nature of the oneness established in the highest moments of friendship or love. But even this concept is not completely adequate to the greatness of this fact, for we are here concerned with the highest experience possible to man. There are no adequate analogies, for all of them would be less than the fact itself. It is the veritable meeting of the deep central reality of ourselves with the actual Spirit of God who visits our heart. We shall consider it more fully as we discuss the Transforming Union. Here let it suffice to point out that it is the highest possible intensity of oneness of our spirit with God's Spirit, but never the destruction of the human personality at any moment of the experience. Man still is experiencing himself as an ultimate entity—"I"; but the "I" is profoundly conscious that it is confronted by and in contact with the Divine Personality, the eternal "Thou," whom it worships, loves, and adores. In its essence this is still an "I-Thou" relationship.

That this is the concept held by Christian mysticism itself is revealed in the famous passage in which Jacob Boehme applies the symbolism of fire to the Transforming Union:

I give you an earthly similitude of this. Behold a bright flaming piece of iron, which of itself is dark and black, and the fire so penetrateth and shineth through the iron, that it giveth light. Now, the iron doth not cease to be; it is iron still: and the source (or property) of the fire retaineth its own propriety: it doth not take the iron into it, but it penetrateth (and shineth) through the iron; and it is iron then as well as before, free in itself: and so also is the source or property of the fire. In such a manner is the soul set in the Deity; the Deity penetrateth through the soul, and dwelleth in the soul, yet the soul doth not comprehend the Deity, but the Deity comprehendeth the soul, but doth not alter it (from being a soul) but only giveth it the divine source (or property) of the Majesty.[3]

c. It Is Not Quietism. While the true mystic recognizes the value of receptivity, of inner stillness, of quieting our self-will, his ideal is not a continuing state of passivity. To believe that mysticism requires us to escape from reality and permanently reduces personal action to a minimum is not the Christian ideal of sanctity and perfection.

In the higher life of devotion we are called to concentrate our attention upon God, to withdraw from our concern with the world; but this is a temporary and purposeful withdrawal. It is climbing the Mount of Transfiguration, but it is not staying there in continuous passivity. Peter's suggestion that the disciples build tabernacles and live permanently upon the mountain was refused by Jesus. He led them back from this high place down into the valley where a man needed the healing power that He brought from God.

One fundamental distinction between Eastern mysticism and Christian mysticism is right here. Christian mysticism always issues in holiness of life, power of action, and effectiveness of influence. We go apart into the high places of prayer in order that we may be empowered for service in the valley of life. As Dean Inge puts it, "The vision is meant, not to be enjoyed, but to be employed."

d. The Ultimate Test Is Its Christlikeness. Any aspect which is not in the Spirit of Christ must be immediately rejected. He is the norm for testing all spiritual experience. The high experiences with which we are now to be concerned must always be character-building, healthy-minded, spiritually integrating, creatively effective, and Christlike.

[3] *The Threefold Life of Man*, VI. 88.

2. ADVANCING TO THE HIGH PLACES OF PRAYER

Many people fear the higher road of prayer because they have confused it with one of the mistaken manifestations of it which we have just discussed. But deep in the heart of all Christians is the impulse to advance toward God. One of the reasons for the development of strange and rootless cults in our day is the inescapable urge in the heart of people to come more closely into contact with God. Frustrated by the failure of the Christian Church to provide balanced guidance and strong, clean counsels of spirituality, they have turned aside to these unsatisfactory substitutes. The Church is failing in its duty when it does not present a way to the heights of the spirit that is founded upon the revelation which we have received in Christ Jesus our Lord. Every Christian should be called continually to advance as far on the road toward God as he possibly can and in every way that he can.

All Christians should have a goal of ultimate development toward which, with God's help, they are seeking continually to progress. The fact that perfection, sanctification, and holiness have been presented in crude and bizarre forms should prompt us, not to reject these ultimate goals which are implicit in the Gospel of Christ, but rather to clarify our conception of them, to present them strongly in their original meanings, and to call all Christians to strive to meet their high demands.

All too many join the church and then feel that just to be average members fulfills their duty as Christians. They attend church with fair regularity. They say their prayers once a day without much change or development over a period of years. They are respectable citizens, and are not guilty of any great moral failures. This, they feel, is what it means to be a Christian. Joining the church, really, is merely matriculating for the disciplines, the training, and the deepening experiences which should keep us growing and reaching to the very end of life. "Not as though I had already attained, either were already made perfect; but ... I press toward the mark for the prize of the high calling of God in Christ Jesus." (Phil. 3:12-14.) There is always more beyond—much more. When a man has awakened to the tremendous spiritual experiences which are his birthright and his calling as a Christian, he will maintain his inner glow by a life of devotion which never ceases to grow deeper and richer.

Sometimes, when we have made a little progress beyond the average, we find ourselves beset with pride, which, whether we know it or not, negates the reality of our advance. In truth, we have not become aware of the ultimate demands that must reach to the very core of our character until every vestige of human pride dies within us. The perfection to which we are called involves a rugged course of pruning in which we root out every un-Christlike attitude within us. It also involves the attainment of every Christlike virtue of which we are capable and the performing of every Christian action for Christ's Kingdom which God wills to accomplish through us. At its very highest it leads us through the ascending ranges of prayer and devotion that bring us to the utmost closeness to God of which we are capable.

These high demands should press in upon us constantly. Indifference and lukewarmness are more deadly sins than we have realized, for they rob God of the channels for mankind's blessing which He seeks through us, and they drug our souls with the self-satisfaction of minor achievements until our high capacities for oneness with God atrophy and die away. Jesus said, "Be ye therefore perfect, even as your Father which is in heaven is perfect." (Matt. 5:48.) This is as real a commandment as any that He ever gave.

Again we are called to follow in His steps in a veritable imitation of Christ. All too often we, like Peter and James and John, have paused at the entrance to the garden of prayer and fallen asleep there. Of Jesus it was said, "He went a little farther, and fell on his face, and prayed." How pathetically far from the heights of the prayer of Gethsemane we have faltered! There is an old gospel hymn which says:

I'll go with Him through the garden,
I'll go with Him through the garden,
I'll go with Him through the garden,
I'll go with Him, with Him all the way.[4]

How pathetically far from "all the way" we have gone as Christians! What cup of self-crucifixion have we ever drunk? What heroic part have we ever taken in the building of His Kingdom? What heights of communion with the Eternal Father have we ever reached? What love like His have we ever felt toward God? This is what life and prayer mean for a Christian, and this secret the saints of the ages, who have most devotedly followed His steps, have always known. And this is the road to which at the climax of prayer we are summoned to advance.

But none of the ransomed ever knew
  How deep were the waters crossed;
Nor how dark was the night that the Lord passed through
  Ere He found His sheep that was lost.[5]

3. THE DARK NIGHT OF THE SOUL

No matter how we conceive of it, there is an ultimate high experience of prayer. It is so tremendous that it is almost impossible to put into words, but its glory is suggested in Jesus' high-priestly prayer in the midnight hour in the Upper Room just before Gethsemane when He prayed "that they all may be one; as thou, Father, art in me, and I in thee, that they also may be one in us; . . . that they may be one, even as we are one: I in them, and thou in me, that they may be made perfect in one." (John 17:21-23.) These words suggest a living and profound oneness at the height of the spiritual life of a man with his God. Certainly to such an experience must uniquely apply the Master's saying: "Strait is the gate, and narrow is the way, which leadeth unto life, and few there be that find it."

[4] E. W. Blandly.
[5] Elizabeth C. Clephane.

(Matt. 7:14.) He calls us to it with full warning of the terrific cost we must pay in adjusting our lives perfectly to the will of God: "If any man will come after me, let him deny himself, and take up his cross, and follow me."

"Prayer," says Emily Herman, "is a dying to self and becoming alive unto God. . . . Each stage of a progressive prayer-life is a stage in the putting to death of the self that God may work and reign." [6] This turning from self-will to God's will, from self-love to God's love, is, as we have seen, one of the four major spiritual movements of the soul toward God. At its height this surrender is so costly that it well deserves the descriptive name John of the Cross gave to it, the Dark Night of the Soul.

At the beginning prayer may still be self-centered. We may want to use it as a means to help us enjoy our material life and its pleasures. As we advance a little in prayer, God becomes more real to us; yet even here we sometimes find that we are but substituting spiritual joys for material pleasures and that the object is still our satisfaction. Self is not dead. We progress to the prayer of contemplation and undergird our spiritual life with more substantial foundations. Our loving attention is more truly centered on God. We are rising toward the consciousness of His nearness. We are experiencing the calm peace of perfect rest in God. Yet even here sometimes it is still self-love that makes us "hug the white peace of God" to our hearts. Now, very gently but firmly, God withdraws this peace and illumination from us for a time. Only then do we realize how truly self had still been in control. Now He leads us to a giving of ourselves to Him with a reality that we had never experienced before. We have come to a climax in the purging of self-centeredness from our lives. We are learning to correct and restrain our desires and even to give our very hearts to Him, at least in the high moments of our contemplation. In doing this we have passed through the first stage of the Dark Night of the Soul.

[6] *Creative Prayer*, p. 100. Used by permission of Harper & Bros.

Now we are being called to a more radical soul-transformation in which our very desires themselves will be remade. We are entering the deeper struggle of the soul as it wrestles to surrender the inner center of its spirit to God. We have come to a place where, in an ultimate relationship, we begin to see the greatness of God over against the evil in ourselves, the divine majesty over against our finite weakness. Suddenly we sense the vast distance that separates the two. Nothing within us is of eternal value save as He upholds us by His grace. Apart from God we are impotent, meaningless, dead. We realize that our powers are futile to bring us to the full knowledge of God. It is not that we abandon reason and become irrational, but rather that we recognize that Reality and our philosophy of reality are two different things. Now we are being drawn to seek humbly for contact with Reality in itself. Our finite thoughts can never be big enough to catch the inexpressible glory of the infinite nature of God. It is God in Himself whom now we seek. We must surrender our pride of intellect as we reach out for our ultimate contact with Reality. Similarly we must give up our feelings, recognizing that in emotional prayer we may be still enjoying ourselves rather than actually questing the Eternal. Even so, our wills must be surrendered so that with utmost purity we desire God and are not misled into ego impulses for our own spiritual enhancement.

We are entering upon the second phase of the Dark Night of the Soul. Of this Emily Herman says:

It is well therefore that after we have made the great dedication, we should be led into that arid twilight land where our schemes miscarry and our judgments mislead us, where emotion withers and will is seen to be but a broken reed, where we grope and totter and fall until we realise how frail was the staff of self upon which we had leaned, and, mistrusting ourselves, learn to put all our confidence in God.[7]

We are being led to a high point of prayer as pure worship and ultimate devotion. Like Isaiah in the temple, we are

[7] *Ibid.*, p. 105. Used by permission of Harper & Bros.

beginning to see the supreme value of God in Himself, high and lifted up, with His train filling the temple. We sense the meaning of the cry of the angels, "Holy, holy, holy, is the Lord of hosts: the whole earth is full of his glory." We too are going out of ourselves in adoration for the Most High. Like the prophet, also, we see the fiery altar where our inmost cleansing is to be accomplished. It is ourselves that we are to present as a living sacrifice, holy, acceptable unto God. In one final and mighty act of devotion and dedication we are to surrender our self-will and our self-love.

The Dark Night of the Soul is the long process of entering into full oneness with God by a progressive surrender of our lives to Him. Classically the term is restricted to denote, in its first phase, the complete giving of ourselves to God during the Prayer of Quiet and, in its most distinctive phase, our ultimate surrender to God on the threshold of the Transforming Union.

All of us who are advancing to the heights of the spirit have entered upon this process. The important thing is not for us to analyze how far we have progressed (thus revealing a subtle lingering of self-centeredness) , but rather to continue with all our hearts to reach toward God in supreme adoration and devotion. We do not seek the darkness; we are in quest of His light. We do not, however, dodge the darkness since this costly struggle is the ultimate way to His Presence. Those who have advanced the farthest toward God tell us that it is not until the last step of the long and difficult way has been taken that God will be able to break through in all the fullness of His glory. Nevertheless we find at every stage of the process that whenever we truly let go of self in sincere surrender, God graciously illumines us with the increasing radiance of His Presence.

4. THE ULTIMATE SURRENDER

When we come to the ultimate surrender, it is the Holy Spirit of God who is operating upon our prepared spirit. "As many as are led by the Spirit of God, they are the sons of God." (Rom. 8:14.) Now God desires to lead us further. We have risen in our devotions to a point where we are enkindled by His love. We have been disciplined for a stronger love than was possible far back at the beginning of our pilgrimage. Now we realize that the soul that has progressed farthest in its love for God must build its will into closest conformity to the will of God. We have pruned away the branches of our desires and pleasures, but the roots from which they developed are still in us. We now sense that our imperfections are rooted in a certain wrongness in our own spirits. We are being called to continue in prayer until we are deeply changed at the very center of our being.

This is a discovery that disturbs us profoundly—yes, the more clearly we understand it, the more deeply does it disturb us. We sense that the inner citadel of our very heart must be given to God. I asked E. Stanley Jones, Muriel Lester, and Kagawa—all separately—"What is the first step in deep prayer?" Each of them answered in one word: "Surrender." When I asked for an explanation of a word that had always seemed negative to me, each, in one way or another, defined surrender in Kagawa's words: "A letting go of self into God." It is a surrender of our will to God's will.

When the Christian mystics speak of self-loss, they do not mean, as we have said, the pantheistic destruction of personality in nirvana. Personality is not to be lost; it will come forth enhanced and enriched, clothed with higher capacities, and lifted to new levels of creative power. But the condition of this advance is the utter destruction of all those elements of our assertive, ego-centered, narrow self which hinder God's mighty and majestic purposes through us. It is the immature ego that must die. To what levels of psychological health we should all rise, if we could thus transcend the idolatrous devotion to our ego image which is the root of inferiority complexes, psychological escape mechanisms, and unhealthy projections of our desires. Here all strivings of self-will must be silenced.

Our narrow and self-centered intentions must be put to death. Our very existence must be given to God. This is a crucifixion of the natural self in order that our deep self, our God-intended self, may be freed to live.

Such a profound soul transformation is a costly and creative process. Our false peace and partial security is given up for God's peace and eternal security. In the flame and fire of this ultimate contact of God's Spirit with ours the habits and imperfections of a lifetime are consumed—habits and imperfections that are so entwined with our surface self that only the mighty power of God could rid us of them. This complete undoing of the self in its very nature leaves us humbled. Pride is at last slain in us, but we have humbled ourselves under the mighty hand of God, that He might exalt us in due season. All through this process of self-stripping we are sustained by the knowledge that it is God who is at work in us, creating for us a far more exceeding weight of glory. Hitherto we have sought our own pleasures and our own purposes because of our great love for ourselves; these are now lost in our greater love for God. God is now loved more than all these things. Our adoration and love for Him have grown so deep that we now retain nothing that would cause Him anxiety.

Any one of us who comprehends the depth of this experience would know that we do not come to it in the early stages of our development. We do not even comprehend what the ultimate divine demand is until we have disciplined ourselves by obedience to the earlier revelations of His will for us. Now in the deeps of our hearts we hear His voice saying, "Son, daughter, give me thy heart."

Anyone who really knows what the ultimate demand of God is must pass through a time of tense suffering and inward pain when the very roots of his psychological nature are being torn up, and he is passing from the immature level to the high maturity of a completely spiritual personality. It is a time of chaos—creative, but chaos nevertheless. It is a time when the very foundations on which he has built his plans and actions

for years tremble beneath the earthquaking experience of
contact with the will of God. It is therefore a time of darkness.
For a while a man seems separated from his friends. They
cannot understand the deeps through which he is passing, and
he has no language—which they would comprehend—through
which to share it with them. He feels empty and impoverished.

Even his joy in spiritual things temporarily is withdrawn.
Hitherto he has in part sought spiritual illumination in
order that his ego might enjoy it. Now he is seeking God in
Himself. The very fact that after all his years of Christian
living and spiritual advance he has not yet attained to a more
permanent oneness with God makes for inner pain. He dimly
apprehends that there is some blessed and mighty experience
of God Himself which is possible for him. Glimpses have come
with strong assurance in his moments of contemplation, glimpses
of God which he cannot doubt. In meditation he has wrestled
with deep thoughts of God and arrived at rugged convictions
of faith, but now he comes to the realization that he has not
made real contact in the very deeps of himself with the very
will of God. There is pain in this knowledge. There is a sense
of frustration. Because he is now reaching for the ultimate,
the lesser no longer satisfies. There is aridity and dryness in his
soul. Because he has not yet attained the vision of God, he
feels alone, bereaved, forsaken. God is there, but lost in a
great cloud of unknowing. God is there, but in the divine
dark he cannot find Him.

For a while he must journey in the dark. An experience,
which by analogy reveals how strange everything appears to
him under these conditions, came to me one time as I was
called to climb in the night from the Lake of the Clouds, high
on the summit of Mount Washington, down the Ammonoosuc
Ravine to the base. It was necessary for me to make the descent
because another person was feared lost on the mountain. The
trail was difficult to discern. The cairns on the upper ridges
and the blazes on the trees below timber line were obscure and
confusing. Once a trail leading off to the left seemed to be a

239

well-worn path, but it led me part way down a dangerous precipice beside a waterfall. I had confused this side trail, which led but to a vantage point above the falls, for the way I should take. When far down the mountainside I had to cross and recross the stream, the footing in the dark was slippery and uncertain, and the steppingstones were difficult to discern. It was a journey dangerous, trying, and confusing, but by following the trail with utmost attention I at last came through safe.

In the dark there have been stars. Somehow, unshakably, we have been confident that God was with us in the dark. It was the depth of our love for Him and the power of the love of His Spirit for us that held us at every step to the high fulfillment of His dream for us. God was freeing us from our lower selves. God was never nearer to us than on this terrible journey, and now, at length, the light of dawn trembles silverly through the dark—and we move through the beauty of the dawn of His Presence into the sunlight of His perfect love.

CHAPTER XVIII

The Flame of Living Love

TRANSFORMING UNION

That they may be one, even as we are one: I in them, and thou in me, that they may be made perfect in one. —John 17:22-23

THE EXPERIENCE OF THE MEETING OF OUR SPIRITS WITH GOD after we have passed through the Dark Night of the Soul constitutes the Transforming Union. It is beyond all other experiences and cannot be described in terms lower than itself. This does not mean that it is a subjective vagary of some individual soul. It is subjective in the sense of being the conscious experience of a person, but it is not subjective in the sense of being opposed to objective reality. It possesses the highest possible validity. It has been validated in the experience of those in all ages and in all nations who have fulfilled its conditions. The extent and unanimity of their testimony cannot be lightly set aside. The fact that man can and does experience God with a tremendous and powerful immediacy is the major hypothesis of the spiritual life. It is as valid as any scientific hypothesis, and it can be verified by any soul who will fulfill the conditions of profundity of faith, holiness of heart, dedication of life, and devotion in prayer.

Neither is it to be deprecated as an abnormal experience, for it moves rather in the realm of the normal, heightened and lifted to its ultimate expression. Only as man struggles up to the summit of his highest intellectual, moral, social, and spiritual achievements can he condition his soul for its most complete contact with God.

It is indescribable only in the sense that it transcends all other experiences so that finding language with which to communicate its fullness is exceedingly difficult. But this is true of any ultimate human experience. How could the Brownings describe love to those who had never loved profoundly? How could Michelangelo describe the creative process in art to one who had never agonized to create a masterpiece? How could Washington describe patriotism to one who had never dedicated his whole life to preserve his country? It is in this sense that high prayer does not yield its ultimate secret to those who have not paid the price of climbing the spiritual summits. But the Transforming Union does have characteristics which can be described, and through them we can catch glimpses of the larger meanings "that slip through language and escape."

1. UNION WITH GOD

We are all enmeshed in eternity all the time, only we have not become aware of it until now. God is interacting with our lives. We are upheld and sustained by His will from the moment of the creation of our souls by Him through every moment that we exist through His grace. Our energy, our lives, and the continuation of our personalities depend upon the great Reality in which we live and move and have our being. As we come to ourselves in a richer and more intense self-discovery, we become aware of our place in the universe and of our relation to God.

At first this is by faith; now it is by sight. We are entering into communication with the Divine Essence itself. We are dwelling within the Eternal. We have entered upon a loving and peaceful state of waiting upon God. The Holy Spirit is acting in the very ground of our soul to reveal the reality of His nearness. We come to know that God is standing over against our life penetrating us with His light and His love. Through the miracle of His grace God is flooding the soul with abundance of light, permitting us to share in the experience of His nature. We are being reborn by the will of God and therefore are becoming sons of God, partakers of the divine nature through God's love and grace, even as was the purpose of the Almighty when He first made man in His own image. We do not confuse the two substances, the divine with the human. It is a union that springs from the heart and will of man, but it is his will as it has been transformed to the will of God. Man freely wills this union as the value which he supremely desires. His whole nature becomes one flame of living love toward God as he reaches out in the high and tremendous experience of contact with his Maker.

John of the Cross, to whose penetrating analyses anyone who seeks to describe the heights of the spirit must return, makes perfectly clear the nature of this union by a comparison:

A ray of sunlight is striking a window. If the window is in any way stained or misty, the sun's ray will be unable to illumine it and transform it into its own light, totally, as it would be if it were clean of all things, and pure; but it will illumine it to a lesser degree, in proportion as it is less free from those mists and stains; and will do so to a greater degree, according as it is cleaner from them, and this will not be because of the sun's rays, but because of itself; so much so that, if it be wholly pure and clean, the ray of sunlight will transform it and illumine it in such wise that it will itself seem to be a ray and will give the same light as the ray. Although in reality the window has a nature distinct from that of the ray itself, however much it may resemble it, yet we may say that that window is a ray of the sun or is light by participation. And the soul is like this window, whereupon is ever beating (or, to express it better, wherein is ever dwelling) this Divine light of the Being of God according to nature, which we have described.[1]

2. THE TRANSFORMATION OF PERSONALITY

All who have attained to this experience become more heroic spiritual figures and live at transcendent levels of reality.

[1] *The Ascent of Mount Carmel,* Book II, ch. v.

The soul is aware of the transforming of its nature in God through love. The elements of man are still the same, but they are as changed as when the carbon in coal becomes the carbon in a diamond. They now gleam and glow with an inner radiance. God is not now merely the object of our devotion. We are conscious that in a mysterious way He is divinely communicating new life to us. He is the Vine, we are the branches. As we have established contact with Him, we feel His energy flowing up through our lives. We are unable to describe the sublimity of this participation in the grace which God is directly bestowing upon us. Our thinking is enriched by the eternal thoughts of God. Our disciplined will is empowered by the direct creative action of the divine will through us. Our love is immeasurably enhanced, not merely by the perception of the divine love, but by its flow into and through our heart. The soul is now habitually conscious of the divine co-operation in all the heights and depths of its being.

No personal union of a more intimate kind can be conceived. God is acting through us. "Yet," says Ruysbroeck, "the creature does not become God, for the union takes place in God through grace and our homeward-turning love; and, therefore, the creature in its inward contemplation feels a distinction and otherness between itself and God." [2] Personality has not been lost; it has only been made more real. As Augustine points out, "When I shall cleave to Thee with all my being, . . . my life shall be a real life, being wholly full of Thee." [3] Man has entered upon a new order of life in which his personality is being remade on higher levels.

This indwelling by God fulfills man's highest potentiality as a child of the Eternal. This action is not different from the action of the Divine at every level of the whole series of creation. Archbishop William Temple has pointed out that

[2] Underhill, *Mysticism*, p. 423.
[3] *Ibid.*, p. 420.

no realm in the universe reveals its full powers, or achieves all that is inherently latent within it, until it is indwelt by the manifestation of the next higher realm above it. Matter in its physicochemical state has certain properties, but matter indwelt by life reveals a whole new group of powers. Again, when life is indwelt by consciousness, the fullness implicit in life finds still more perfect expression. And still again, when conscious life, or personality, is indwelt by the Divine Personality, its potential height is revealed. There are no yawning chasms that cut one realm off from the next. The whole world is so planned that the influence of the higher can enter into and transform the lower. There is no absolute gulf between human personality and divine personality. The very incarnation of Christ, which is the central heart of our faith, gives ground for the daring assumption that man is akin to God.

3. CERTITUDE

As we are thus united to God, and our personalities are transformed into His likeness and opened to the divine activity upon us, God is enabled to communicate to us the highest spiritual graces. The first of these is an inner certitude growing out of the experience of the fact of His Presence. As we lingered in the obscurity of the Dark Night of the Soul, there came to us, beyond and above our control, the dawning of the consciousness of the mysterious Presence of God. We had risen to the highest and purest attention of which we were capable; we had attained an intensity of perception even beyond the synoptic vision of our earlier contemplation. We had equipped ourselves, through the struggles in the dark, with soul strength to realize God. Our own will was purified and silenced. We awaited His coming. We knew that we were resting upon and abiding within the eternal world where God is. Then to us came the apprehension of a profound contact with God.

Now, in the Transforming Union, overwhelmed by the conviction of being so close to God that we have broken through into His very Presence, we say in awed wonder like Isaiah in the temple: "I saw the Lord." It is a dazzling experience of eternity. It is an overwhelming sense of being in touch with the absolute Source of all that is. There is the thrilling sense of the inflow of the divine love. God is with us in a way that convinces us of this fact forever. God has caused us to feel His Presence.

God has appeared to the soul under a new aspect, as a living Reality, grasped by a sort of experimental knowledge far beyond the limits of deduction and induction. Most frequently, the first time we experience the Transforming Union, it is the Living Christ who reveals Himself to the soul. Through the time-transcending grace of God, the miracle of Easter is repeated within us. Then the Holy Spirit illumines the mind, leading us into all truth. And at length the Presence of the infinite Creator dawns upon us.

We are confused and overawed by our closeness to the greatness of the God-heart. Our littleness trembles in the Presence of His Almightiness. We are in the Presence of the Holy God, who swings the stars in their courses and holds the unthinkable spaces of the universe in His hands, and yet He has stooped in gracious condescension to us as we worship before Him. Then we experience the blessed Trinity all at once, sensing the flaming love that unites God's being in eternal oneness, and yet aware of the infinite richness and reality of the wonder of the Father, the Son, and the Holy Spirit. God is directing our inner apprehension of a greatness beyond our power to grasp without His aid. He is imparting to us revelations of naked truth. The soul is aware of sublime intellectual perceptions of God. It cries out in the language of John: "We shall be like him, for we shall see him as he is."

We no longer need be satisfied with the love that filters through the crevices of the door; we have had glimpses of the eternal glory. God has penetrated the citadel of our souls. We have been so near to God that we are transformed in the flame of His love. Our awesome emotion in the Presence of God's transcendence imperceptibly deepens into the adoration of our love. We are aware of His nearness and His intimacy. Reality is a Person and not a state. We are in a universe of personality, and to us by His graciousness the Divine Personality has spoken.

This experience of God is not an exterior locution; we hear no outer voices. It is not an imaginary locution; the imagination has been purged away, and we are far beyond the realm of all sense imagery. It is rather an intellectual locution or apprehension. It is a simple and direct communication from God to our souls. He has not infused into us the abstractions of theology; His aim is a more practical one. He has revealed Himself in love. He has manifested Himself as a majestic and mighty fact of experience. He has fused us into inner reverence and holiness of heart. He has energized our will for mighty achievement through the powerful action of His Spirit. None who have ever had this visitation from on high can ever doubt its validity. It becomes the central fact by which all other facts are tested. We are indeed convinced by it forever.

4. THE INFLOW OF DIVINE POWER

This tremendous experience opens new channels in us for the inflow of divine power. As the soul is transformed in God, it becomes aware of a new, amazing inner strength. It no longer must divide its own limited power in an effort to help others; it is aware of the mighty tide of divine action pouring into it and through it. God is acting. The soul is summoned to a loving co-operation with God's creative action. It is willing to dare anything to please Him. It cries out, "Here am I, send me." It comes to understand that a great part in the drama of creation is given to the free spirit of man. Being closer to God, the soul becomes a humble channel through which God's intentions for others can flow. This is the essential characteristic of Christian mysticism. It is always creative and productive. Its great spirits are characterized by heroic effort and creative activity. How clearly now we see that the Transforming Union is not the suppression of personality but its perfecting, its vitalizing, and its intensification!

The supreme effect of the Transforming Union is to produce a unique fruitfulness in our life. We become an actual center of spiritual vitality to other men. There is a law whereby those who have climbed to the height of this experience are made powerful to influence others. They beget many spiritual children. They communicate the divine life to others. They are so radiant with the fire of the divine that they illumine and enkindle those about them, though often they are entirely unaware that they are doing this and always they are characterized by profound humility. They are not content merely to enjoy the light of God which they sense; they must share the new radiance with all others. This is why great Christian mystics, saints, and men and women of prayer have been the great missionaries, evangelists, philanthropists, poets, prophets, and servants of mankind. Some of the most virile souls among them have influenced the destinies of nations. They become the medium by which God's life flows out into His world.

5. THE PRACTICE OF THE PRESENCE OF GOD

An experience as powerful as this produces an impact upon the human personality that is permanent. Henceforth the abiding environment of our life is the Presence of God. This does not mean that we withdraw from the world of time and space and human experience. We live normally, a part of all that goes on around us, but far in the deeps of our spirit there is a constant recollection of God. This persists even amid our external occupations. While earlier in contemplation we have begun to practice His Presence, now we do this to a far greater degree.

There is an inner security that is unshakable, for God Himself leads us. We are radiant, for we are being constantly illumined from within. We are unified, for we are integrated about God as our life center and are responsive to the lightest whisper of His will. We abide in love, for "he that dwelleth in love dwelleth in God, and God in him." (I John 4:16.) There is within us a permanent intellectual awareness of God to which we return continually. We are no longer strangers and far off; we are at home in the universe; we belong; we are living; we have entered into oneness with God.

This does not mean that there is any artificial sense of human perfection. Our experience may suffer a temporary eclipse, but if we have paid the price of really passing through the Dark Night of the Soul, the interruption is of short duration. In our actions the spiritual soul is in charge, and as long as God's grace upholds us we shall not willfully sin. But we know that it is only through the continuous practice of His Presence and the eternal manifestation of His grace that we shall be preserved from imperfections and failures. The grace of the Transforming Union could not have been given to us until the discipline and purification of our life had been sincerely undertaken.

The practice of the Christian virtues always precedes the gift of the spiritual graces. As long as self-will, pride, or any of the seven deadly sins remain in control of our lives, God could not endow us, nor trust us, with this heightened life. One of the absolute tests of our progress in the spiritual life is the absence of spiritual pride. Those who speak too assertively about their spiritual advance, or strive too dogmatically to tell others how to improve their religious lives, or make claims concerning their own perfection, holiness, or sanctification, pathetically demonstrate how small a distance they have traveled on the true path that leads to the Presence of God.

Again, the Transforming Union does not come and go with the unpredictability of our transient experiences of God in earlier contemplation. It has made such a profound impact upon our lives that its influence can never pass away. Then, too, once God has given it to us, it is not readily withdrawn. Only the failure of our whole soul structure in some crumbling moral disaster can negate this experience once it is sincerely and really attained after self-will is truly dead. If our very heart of hearts has been surrendered to the action of the Most High, then we abide under the shadow of the Almighty.

Always the background of our life is God. Life is reoriented about the Divine, and daily living is carried forward under the guidance of His will. In deepest reality we now are enabled to practice the Presence of God. Humbly, reverently, quietly, sincerely, we live in awed dependence upon Him.

The experience of the Transforming Union in its fullness and in its permanence comes only at the height of our spiritual pilgrimage after we have fully passed through the Dark Night of the Soul. Nevertheless, through the grace of God we are again and again lifted into its forecourts through our experiences in the Prayer of Active Contemplation. We experience foretastes of the ineffable glory of the Divine Presence even though the experience is transient and partial. The Holy Spirit of God grants us gracious anticipations of the radiant fullness toward which we progressively journey.

We began this book with a picture of Christ waiting to conduct the symphony of God's eternal purpose. Here at the climax of prayer we, His children, glimpse the possibility of joining in the ultimate harmony. If what we have been saying is true—and the experience of the greatest Christians of all ages attests its truth unmistakably—then the real Kingdom of God is now waiting for the co-operation of awakened souls, men and women who dare to climb the heights toward God. It is waiting for us. "Lord, teach us to pray."

INDEX